CW00696518

# Microsoft®
# Flight
# Simulator

## By Brittany Vincent

A Wiley Brand

## Microsoft® Flight Simulator For Dummies®

Published by: **John Wiley & Sons, Inc.,** 111 River Street, Hoboken, NJ 07030-5774, www.wiley.com

Copyright © 2023 by John Wiley & Sons, Inc., Hoboken, New Jersey

Published simultaneously in Canada

For general information on our other products and services, please contact our Customer Care Department within the U.S. at 877-762-2974, outside the U.S. at 317-572-3993, or fax 317-572-4002. For technical support, please visit https://hub.wiley.com/community/support/dummies.

Wiley publishes in a variety of print and electronic formats and by print-on-demand. Some material included with standard print versions of this book may not be included in e-books or in print-on-demand. If this book refers to media such as a CD or DVD that is not included in the version you purchased, you may download this material at http://booksupport.wiley.com. For more information about Wiley products, visit www.wiley.com.

Library of Congress Control Number: 2023930716

ISBN 978-1-119-82845-7 (pbk); ISBN 978-1-119-82846-4 (ePDF); ISBN 978-1-119-82847-1 (ePub)

Printed and bound by CPI Group (UK) Ltd, Croydon, CR0 4YY

C9781119828457_011223

# Contents at a Glance

# Table of Contents

# Introduction

H ave you ever wanted to fly around the world simply by booting up a video game? Stop over at some of the largest airports in the country, then zip around to the other side of the globe with a plane full of passengers?

Welcome to Microsoft Flight Simulator 2020, the most realistic flying simulation game on the market. You're not confined to a single map or two, or even an incomplete list of destinations. The world is your oyster, as they say. And you can go anywhere. Fly from point A to point B, wherever your heart desires, in the confines of this expansive, lovingly crafted game.

But unless you're an actual pilot, a flight simulator expert, or one of the developers, you might need a little help getting started. This isn't like your typical first-person shooter or adventure game. The aircraft you find throughout the book are real-world aircraft. People go to school for years to learn how to fly them.

So with this book, I'm taking you to flight school, so to speak. After you read the parts that are pertinent to your Flight Simulator journey, you can simply jump into the airplane of your choice, spin the globe to choose a destination, and fly there in no time.

Like the wise Joshua Michael Homme of Queens of the Stone Age once sang:

*It's gonna be smooth sailing*
*From here on out*

## About This Book

When you fire up Flight Simulator, it's easy to feel overwhelmed. What do you do first? How in the heck does a plane actually work? Will you ever get off of the runway, and how will you accomplish that? What's the best place to start?

Here's the honest truth: The game won't hold your hand. That's fine. I'm here to do just that. This book is for anyone who has questions, concerns, or frustrations about Flight Simulator. Enjoying a flight simulator game should be for everyone, not just for those with the patience to watch dozens of piecemeal YouTube videos or complete a slew of practice flights.

Really, the *For Dummies* series is all about giving you just what you need to know to accomplish things as simply as possible. In the case of Flight Simulator, you can find out the basics (and handy shortcuts) of the game that can help you fly your favorite aircraft across the world to any destination you choose.

This book is a reference tool crafted to help you get as much out of this realistic simulator as possible. Follow the part and chapter structure to

>> Get acquainted with the nuts and bolts of the game, its setup, and its controls.

>> Find out about basic flight principles that apply in the real world, how to invite friends to fly with you, and even how to play in virtual reality.

>> Pull off a successful start-up and takeoff, and then figure out how to navigate, as well as return to the runway. (Talk about a round-trip flight!)

>> Determine how to find your way around an airport and communicate with air traffic controllers.

>> Select the airplanes that you want to fly with, explore how to navigate while in the air, and embrace flight rules and radio etiquette.

>> Discover the unexpected happenings that can occur when you're in the cockpit, prepare for them, and tackle that emergency landing when you need to.

>> Follow the steps provided to take sample flights in aircraft that have various levels of complexity.

Sure, you could do a few Google searches to find some of the information presented in this book, but there's nothing quite like having everything you need to know gathered in one place. There's still something to be said about a physical tome that contains a wealth of knowledge about a subject.

Consult it when you have no Internet connectivity. Read it when you're on the throne. Roll it up and swat a fly with it. No matter how you slice it, there are about a zillion ways this book can help you inside and outside of Flight Simulator. In a pinch, you could probably use it as an emergency ration. Chewy, but it's still sustenance.

TIP

Buying this book is the cheapest way to consult an expert, really. For less than the price of the game itself, you're getting the expertise of someone who's played video games for nearly 30 years, written about them for almost two decades, and accumulated real-world aviation information as it relates to the aircraft you'll be flying. It's a win for everyone, in my book. This one, I mean.

# Foolish Assumptions

Most level-headed people don't like to make assumptions. But if I wanted to get this book into the hands of those who might need it most, I had to do just that. And here you are, just as planned — which is great! So, let me put it to you like this: If one of these assumptions ends up being incorrect, I have a sneaking suspicion you can still find this book helpful.

I assume that

» **You probably like planes.** Maybe you're interested in their inner workings. Perhaps you enjoy traveling. Either way, you have some sort of rudimentary knowledge or passion about aircraft that makes you want to dive into this book. You might even be a pilot in real life, looking to take your passion into the digital world.

Whatever the case may be, you take some sort of delight in watching, riding in, studying, or looking at planes. Or at the very least, you know what a plane *is*. Right? Okay, great.

» **You're familiar with video games.** You've either played a few of them or you've seen them in passing. You have an interest in video gaming, even if you're not an avid gamer. Whether you've killed a few Goombas here and there, or explored Magicant several times over, gaming is at least a small part of your life.

» **You're curious about or enjoy simulation games.** Maybe you've driven everything from farm equipment to trains in the digital world, and planes are the next frontier. (Great choice, by the way.) It seems obvious to me that you enjoy either the idea of flying an aircraft or the actual experience. The thrill of seeing the world from 40,000 feet in the air never wears off — in the real world or in the game.

REMEMBER

So whether you're a hardcore gamer who happens to enjoy sim games or you're an aspiring pilot looking to get a little virtual practice in before you actually hop in the cockpit, you can get something out of this book. And if not, well, go ahead and buy it anyway. Collecting retro tech is getting expensive, and I'm still trying to add a Super Lady Cassette Vision from Epoch Co. and a copy of *Milky Princess* to my stores.

# Icons Used in This Book

Need a wingman? I'm right here! Well, I'm here spiritually, in the form of icons, anyway. Throughout this book, icons in the margins highlight certain types of valuable information that call out for your attention. Here are the icons you encounter and a brief description of each.

The Tip icon marks tips and shortcuts that you can use to make it much easier to navigate your first flight, set up multiplayer sessions, understand how some of the game's aircraft differ, and more.

Remember icons mark the information that's especially important to know. Want to know the most important tidbits from each chapter? Just skim through these icons, and you'll be flying fancy free in no time.

The Technical Stuff icon marks information of a highly technical nature that you can normally skip over. Of course, much of what you can expect out of Microsoft Flight Simulator 2020 often veers into the nitty-gritty, so it can be helpful to stop by and read over some of this content — even if it's just because you're curious.

The Warning icon tells you to watch out! It marks important information that may save you headaches, failed first flights, or overall frustration with the sim. I've got your back — but you don't have a ton of these icons around to worry about.

# Beyond the Book

In addition to the abundance of information and guidance related to Flight Simulator that I provide in this book, you get access to even more help and information online at Dummies.com. Check out this book's online Cheat Sheet by accessing www.dummies.com and searching for "Microsoft Flight Simulator 2020 For Dummies Cheat Sheet."

Online, you can find a quick reference guide to common controls, taking to the skies, and more, all to read over if you don't happen to have the complete book handy. The Cheat Sheet can definitely come through for you in a pinch.

Need help beyond this book and its online information? Don't hesitate to head to YouTube and check out the many talented creators who have painstakingly recorded video tutorials that complement the written ones in this book to help you along. You can find a massive Flight Simulator community out there that wants you to spread your wings. You never have to fly alone!

# Where to Go from Here

Just like the aircraft that inspired Flight Simulator, this book is built to take you anywhere you want to go. You can fly through this book however you want because it's not meant to be a linear experience. You can explore and skip around as much as you like as often as you like.

If you need help getting started, feel free to jump in and follow the beginner's tips or check out a sample flight. For those completely new to the Flight Simulator franchise, acclimate yourself to the game with Chapter 1. Also, be sure to check out Chapter 3 for an overview of menus and flight preparations so that you can get a handle on them before jumping into the cockpit.

If you already have a good idea of what to expect from the game, check out Chapter 19 for a master class in breaking down some of the coolest parts of the game. Also, for a selection of interesting airport destinations in-game, take a look at Chapter 19. That way, you don't have to search very long for a destination. The choice can feel overwhelming — because you have the whole world in your hands, quite literally!

If you only really need a quick reference in terms of mouse and keyboard controls or controller support, I have those for you in Chapter 2. You can find everything you need to know about using one or both methods to control Flight Simulator in this chapter, whether you're opting for a hybrid model or sticking strictly to your controller.

It's really up to you how you begin your journey. But know that no matter where you start, I'm here with you every step of the way. Spread your wings and get ready to greet the horizon! The whole world is at your doorstep. You just need to hop into the cockpit and fly there. It really is that easy.

# 1

# Getting Started with Microsoft Flight Simulator

Get a crash course on flight simulators, an overview of the Microsoft Flight Simulator 2020 offerings, and a guide for evaluating and choosing a version of the game.

Find out about selecting the game's control platform and the extensive list of controls for your chosen interface — whether PC keyboard or Xbox controller.

Explore the game's main menu, find good advice and tutorials to guide your flying, and start out right with preparations for takeoff and landing.

Take a look at the preparations and equipment needed to fly a plane in virtual reality.

Discover how to gather your friends, create a multiplayer flight session, get your group flight off the ground, and even troubleshoot your online connectivity.

IN THIS CHAPTER

» Introducing Microsoft Flight
Simulator 2020

» Exploring the history of flight
simulators

» Figuring out whether Microsoft
Flight Simulator 2020 is right
for you

» Choosing a version of Microsoft
Flight Simulator 2020

Chapter **1**

# Taking to the Virtual Skies

A re you ready to see the entire world without leaving your seat? Jump into the cockpit with Microsoft Flight Simulator 2020, and you can do just that. From flying over the majestic Grand Canyon to touring the rolling hills of the town you grew up in, your virtual journey soars. You can truly see it all within the confines of this extraordinary simulation game (sim). A *sim game* is designed to closely simulate a real-world activity — in the case of Flight Simulator, the activity of flying in the aircraft of your choice, at your leisure. You don't even have to worry about the weather.

Many of us will never set foot in a cockpit and are, instead, content to be passengers aboard commercial flights enroute to various destinations. That's by choice for some, or by circumstance for others. Giving people a chance to fly without all the time, money, and risk that goes into actual piloting makes flight simulators such a fun and rewarding experience. Flight Simulator is currently the best of its kind for casual players and hardcore enthusiasts alike. Not only does it let you fly just about anywhere in the world that you want, but you can do it in a dizzying number of different aircrafts, including jetliners and prop planes aplenty, all modeled after their real-world counterparts.

Whether you're a rookie pilot or a seasoned professional, this chapter offers foundation and guidance as you prepare to soar through the friendly skies. It's smooth sailing (or flying) from here on out.

# Following the Evolution of Flight Simulators

Flight simulators sprang up in the early 1900s, and military pilots used them throughout World War I and World War II. As passenger flight became common, civilian pilots would also begin relying on simulators to learn the basics before graduating to a real airplane. Original flight simulators primarily took the form of analog cockpits which were used to train professional pilots and maintenance crews during simulators' early days. As technology evolved, flight simulators transitioned to a more cost-effective digital format that both professionals and enthusiasts could use.

## The Microsoft Flight Simulator that was

In terms of Microsoft's line of flight simulators, the company released Microsoft Flight Simulator 1.0 for the IBM PC in November 1982. This somewhat rudimentary debut used simplistic graphics (as shown in Figure 1-1) but employed systems that included variable weather and time of day, as well as a coordinates system to help players navigate.

**REMEMBER**

The original Flight Simulator game was touted as extremely realistic, offering "full-color, out-the-window flight display" as a draw for those interested in jumping aboard. Only four colors were on display at one time, and the graphics were simplistic depictions known as *vector graphics*. These two visual limitations make the original Flight Simulator look positively archaic when compared to even the most rudimentary video game of the modern industry. The modern version of the game offers photographic realism as well as an amazing number of airports and aircrafts you can choose from.

The original release severely limited the aircraft types and available terrain that you could fly over. Players could board a Cessna 182 (the only plane available in the main game mode) and fly around four areas of the United States: Los Angeles, Chicago, New York City, or Seattle. Players would begin in Chicago's Meigs Field airport, which would continue to be the default starting airport over the years, even as Flight Simulator continued to grow and evolve as an eventual series.

**FIGURE 1-1:**
Microsoft Flight
Simulator 1.0,
released in
November
1982 for the
IBM PC.

Another in-game mode, Europe 1917, let players take flight with a Sopwith Camel plane (a fighter plane, vintage WWI) in a mountainous area, then declare war and grapple with other enemy aircrafts. Although it was an extremely rudimentary simulator, it served as a great foundation for what was to eventually come. Mostly incremental updates happened over the intervening two years, and 1984 marked the release of Microsoft Flight Simulator 2.0. A third sequel appeared four years later in 1988: Microsoft Flight Simulator 4.0.

Numbered updates would continue through 1996, when Flight Simulator for Windows 95 debuted — but beyond that, releases were marked by years rather than versions. Check out the nearby sidebar, "A 30,000-foot view of releases," for a rundown of the evolutionary path taken by Flight Simulator.

## The Microsoft Flight Simulator that is

Flight Simulator is the first release in the series since 2006's Microsoft Flight Simulator X, marking a 14-year absence for the popular game. This new version is also the most feature-rich, with thousands of airports to visit, hundreds of aircrafts, and real-world topographic mapping that allows players to fly around the world at their leisure. It's impressive stuff, to be sure. Figure 1-2 shows an excellent example of the stunning visuals.

## A 30,000-FOOT VIEW OF RELEASES

For the techy audience who cares, here's a complete list of Microsoft Flight Simulator releases over the years, since the beginning:

- Microsoft Flight Simulator 1.0 (1982)
- Microsoft Flight Simulator 2.0 (1984)
- Microsoft Flight Simulator (Mac) (1986)
- Microsoft Flight Simulator 3.0 (1988)
- Microsoft Flight Simulator 4.0 (1989)
- Microsoft Flight Simulator 5.0 (1993)
- Microsoft Flight Simulator 5.1 (1995)
- Microsoft Flight Simulator for Windows 95 (1996)

- Microsoft Flight Simulator 98 (1997)
- Microsoft Flight Simulator 2000 (1999)
- Microsoft Flight Simulator 2002 (2001)
- Microsoft Flight Simulator 2004: A Century of Flight (2003)
- Microsoft Flight Simulator X (2006)
- Prepar3D (2010)
- Microsoft Flight Simulator 2020 (2020)

**Note:** Prepar3D is essentially a branch of Flight Simulator X, brought to market by Lockheed Martin. After the company bought the rights to Prepar3D, it became a separate simulator in its own right. Many Flight Simulator X developers went on to work on Prepar3D after Microsoft closed developer Aces Game Studio.

**FIGURE 1-2:**
One of Flight Simulator promotional screenshots.

*Used with permission from Microsoft.*

Comparing Figure 1-1 to Figure 1-2 shows just how far the game's realistic appearance has come in a relatively short time. Flight simulation has just about reached parity with real-world flight, and in a few years, simulations might offer graphics on par with what you see when you look out the window of an actual plane's cockpit. And with the Flight Simulator experience as immersive as it is right now, I'm anxious to see how much the game improves going forward.

# Evaluating Whether Microsoft Flight Simulator 2020 Is Right for You

When people think of flight simulators, some may tend to envision video games where you simply "fly planes." Sure, that's what you're doing in the end, but Flight Simulator has a lot more to it. Consider this: You can fly planes in arcade-centric games such as the Ace Combat series, but all you really control are aircraft movements (up, down, left, and right), deploying missiles, and laying down gunfire. You control the planes in games like Ace Combat much like you control any other video game avatar. (A game *avatar* is the player character's digital representation.)

## Recognizing that you have much to learn

You get the most out of Flight Simulator when you're interested in figuring out the inner workings of flight and want to enjoy navigating from the perspective of a pilot.

These inner workings include

>> Selecting the types of aircrafts you want to pilot.

>> Doing what you need to do to arrange for takeoff.

>> Understanding how to maintain altitude while flying.

>> Knowing how to maneuver the craft in the air.

>> Finding out how to navigate to your destination.

>> Training to land safely and smoothly on runways across the globe.

REMEMBER

Flight Simulator offers a virtual experience of applying essential flying skills, all while you're chatting with air traffic controllers and multitasking in a way that requires your full attention at all times.

Gaining the knowledge and honing the skills to engage with Flight Simulator is an acquired taste, that's for sure. The process may be frustrating at times, even with the right amount of in-game assistance, tutorials, and this book. In fact, the effort required to understand a real flying skill before applying it in the game may not be fun for some folks. But I find few things more rewarding than jumping into Flight Simulator, getting to know the cockpit, and unraveling the mysteries that come along with becoming a pilot.

TIP

If you're not particularly interested in diving into the most granular parts of flight — including what all those buttons and switches do — you might find that the Flight Simulator game isn't really for you. Keep in mind that it's called a *simulator,* after all; it's meant to be as similar as possible to the real thing.

## Making the decision to tackle Microsoft Flight Simulator

If hopping into a cockpit behind the seemingly inscrutable wall of controls isn't something that appeals to you, you might want to pick up a game with a more arcade-centric approach to flight. That way, you get the fun parts of navigating the skies without the real-world parts you aren't as interested in. If you don't like the idea of a game that expects you to learn more than you want to, don't fret. You can find plenty of other games out there to play.

The most important consideration for delving into Flight Simulator is believing that you can have fun and enjoy yourself throughout what can be hours of figuring out and perfecting the art of flying aircraft. If you're staying the course, I'm happy to have you come take this adventure with me! You can come away with useful knowledge, and you may even achieve a deeper appreciation for what pilots do on a daily basis!

# Selecting and Purchasing Microsoft Flight Simulator

Currently, you can purchase three different versions of Flight Simulator: the Standard, Deluxe, and Premium Deluxe editions. Differences among editions include the number and type of available airports and aircraft, and of course, the price. *Note:* Even the Standard version of Flight Simulator includes around 37,000 airports! Other good news is that the game is largely the same across platforms (PC and Xbox series), so you won't compromise the experience when it comes to choosing the platform you want to play on.

# What platforms can you use to play the game?

Flight Simulator originally debuted as a PC-only title when it first released in August 2020. It also received a special virtual-reality version in December 2020, the first time any flight simulator had done so. Though it remained a PC exclusive title for some time, on July 27, 2021, Flight Simulator debuted on Xbox Series X and Xbox Series S.

The game likely won't be available on PlayStation 4, PlayStation 5, or Nintendo Switch in the near future, given that it's a Microsoft-owned property. So if you're interested in playing, you need to have a PC or Xbox series platform. Here are a couple of thoughts for your platform choice:

» **On Xbox:** You may find that picking up an Xbox console (if you don't already have one) makes playing the game simpler. Flight Simulator is highly playable on Xbox consoles and may be more accessible there for those who aren't comfortable configuring PC games and software.

» **On PC:** Flight Simulator can be quite demanding on computers that don't have pricey gaming equipment. On the other hand, you can expect awesome graphics if you play on a gaming PC that has the latest and greatest graphic card and processor.

# Which version should you buy?

Each version of Flight Simulator differs in scope of content, such as airplanes and airports. The versions (depicted in Figure 1-3) are priced in tiers, and depending on the experience you want from the game, you can expect more or less content based on how much you're willing to pay. Hey, becoming a pilot isn't cheap!

Here's a quick reference guide to what each version contains:

» **Standard Edition:** The base version of the game. It comes with 20 different planes and 30 enhanced airports, and it retails for $59.99 USD.

» **Deluxe Edition:** This version of the game comes with everything in the Standard Edition, plus 5 additional enhanced airports and 5 additional airplanes. It retails for $89.99 USD.

*Enhanced airports included*

- Amsterdam Airport Schiphol (Netherlands)
- Cairo International Airport (Egypt)

FIGURE 1-3:
An infographic
showing
each of Flight
Simulator
unique
versions.

Used with permission from Microsoft.

- Cape Town International Airport (South Africa)

- O'Hare International Airport (USA)

- Adolfo Suarez Madrid-Barajas Airport (Spain)

*Additional airplanes included*

- Diamond Aircraft DA40-TDI

- Diamond Aircraft DV20

- Textron Aviation Inc. Beechcraft Baron G58

- Textron Aviation Inc. Cessna 152 Aerobat

- Textron Aviation Inc. Cessna 172 Skyhawk

» **Premium Deluxe Edition:** This version of the game comes with everything that the Deluxe Edition includes, as well as 5 additional enhanced airports and 5 additional airplanes. It retails for $119.99 USD.

*Enhanced airports included*

- Denver International Airport (USA)

- Dubai International Airport (UAE)

- Frankfurt Airport (Germany)

- Heathrow Airport (UK)

- San Francisco International Airport (USA)

*Additional planes included*

- Boeing Company 787-10 Dreamliner
- Cirrus Aircraft SR22
- Pipistrel Virus SW 121
- Textron Aviation Inc. Cessna Citation Longitude
- Zlin Aviation Shock Ultra

**TIP**

If you decide that you want to upgrade to the Deluxe or Premium Deluxe editions later on, you just have to pay the difference on the platform of your choice. You can download the additional content you were missing to the installation you already have. No pressure!

## Wait, what are enhanced airports?

Don't confuse the small number of enhanced airports in the different versions of the game with the total number of airports that you can fly out of (around 37,000). More enhanced airports come with the Deluxe and Premium Deluxe versions, which means you get adapted constructions of airports (for example, Chicago O'Hare) that are more true-to-life than what they'd normally be in-game.

Game designers handcraft an *enhanced airport* from the ground up to look exactly like the locations in question; the standard, procedurally generated airports aren't nearly as detailed. So if you have a soft spot in your heart for the San Francisco International Airport, you might want to pick up the version of the game that includes its enhanced version so that you can see it just like it looks in your mind's eye. The enhanced airports may end up making it a much more exciting game to jump into — and you want to get the most out of your money, of course!

## What do you need to get started?

Depending on which version of Flight Simulator you plan on playing, the answer to what you need varies. For the most part, whether you're playing on PC, Xbox Series X, or Xbox Series S, you need only a copy of the game, your platform of choice, and some type of input. Your input can be a mouse and keyboard, game controller (I recommend an Xbox controller if you have one), or flight stick. Obviously, you can find a wide variety of all these things. But if you want to use a controller, you can simply use the Xbox gamepad that comes with your Xbox Series X or Xbox Series S by default.

Otherwise, you need your sense of adventure and a little patience. Rome wasn't built in a day. You can't earn your fictional pilot's license in a day, either. You have a lot to learn, but don't get discouraged. As with all things, practice makes perfect, and the more time you spend learning to fly, the more you retain. The more you retain, the better you perform. The better you perform, the more you want to fly. And then, before you know it, you might want to try your luck behind the controls of a real plane! *You* might want to; not me. I'm still a little too terrified. Heights are not my thing.

TIP

You're more than welcome to use a flight stick with your Flight Simulator game if you choose to. I cover the various control methods in Chapter 2. There I describe how you can enjoy your time in the air by using a mouse and keyboard, or a compatible controller. But make no mistake — flight sticks will certainly add another layer of realism to the game and make things all the more exciting when you get the hang of flying.

# Time for the Big Handoff

Flight Simulator is a deep and nuanced simulator. It offers varying experiences for either those who want to figure out how to fly for real or players who just want to see the world in an accessible manner. This chapter helps you get familiar with what the game offers, platforms where you can play it, what version to go for, and even a bit of history of the games themselves. Now, look ahead and get ready to rise into the air.

Get ready, get set, and jump right into the basics. You're going to make a great pilot.

IN THIS CHAPTER

» Setting up your flights just the way
you want them

» Controlling your cockpit by using a
keyboard

» Using a game controller to get a
handle on flying

Chapter **2**

# Taking Control with (or without) a Custom Setup

Microsoft Flight Simulator 2020 offers a lot of room for players to make the game theirs. One important way to customize your flying experience involves making your own cockpit and setup. Although the game is openly supported on Xbox One, Xbox Series X/S, and Xbox Cloud Gaming, even if you're playing on a PC, you can create fully customized cockpits complete with pedals, joysticks, and more.

In this chapter, you can find (many) tables listing the keys, buttons, and combinations that enable you to control your aircraft's lights, cameras, and actions. Getting familiar with these controls should help you prepare to fly the friendly skies, whether you go by mouse and keyboard, or by controller. You can find a control scheme that fits whatever you're looking to get out of the game, whether that's a fully realized sim experience or a fun, casual flight from point A to point B.

For this chapter, I focus more on the controls and systems available to everyone — regardless of whether you have a custom cockpit or setup. However, if you're running a custom cockpit or setup, Flight Simulator gives you complete control to customize how you play your game, including the controls that you use to move around the game world.

# Checking Out Custom Setups and Cockpits

If you decide to tackle customizing how you interface with Flight Simulator, don't worry about replicating an entire cockpit (as shown in Figure 2-1). Most people start with a flight stick or yoke, and then move on to throttles and pedals. However, the sky is the limit, and many hobbyists have created 1-to-1 replicas of the cockpit of their favorite aircraft.

**FIGURE 2-1**
Your cockpit is one of the most important places during your flight.

**WARNING**

Of course, creating custom setups can be time consuming and cost you a good chunk of money, too. But if you really want to make your plane your own, you can customize your flying environment to take your simming to the next level.

## Getting comfortable on consoles

If you're playing on an Xbox console, then you're going to need to get used to using a controller. Although you can find some flight sticks that support Xbox consoles, most of them only support PCs. Because a controller has a limited number of input options compared to a keyboard, you find that many actions require a combination of buttons. For example, when flying with a controller only, you must use RB+Up or Down on the D-Pad to control your trim.

However, you can use a keyboard and mouse versus console if you desire. You can set keybinds (actions assigned to a key or key combination) on Xbox exactly the same way you can on PC. You can even use a combo of controller and keyboard and mouse if you prefer.

## Perfect PC controls

On a PC, the controls are a bit more spread out, thanks to the massive amount of buttons available on a standard keyboard. Because Flight Simulator utilizes almost every key on the keyboard, I highly recommend that you play the game by using a complete keyboard (one that includes a separate number pad, or *numpad*, for example). If you use a smaller keyboard — 60 percent or smaller than a standard keyboard — you get fewer keys.

REMEMBER

Using a full keyboard — one that includes a separate numpad — is ideal because you use several of the keys on the numpad by default for keybinds that help you control the various functions in your aircraft. Alternatively, you could purchase a separate USB numpad. Check out the section "Running the Cockpit from the Keyboard," later in this chapter, for tables hosting the keybinds that help you fly your aircraft if you're using a PC.

## Preparing for virtual reality flights

If you want to take your simulations to an entirely new level of immersion, then Flight Simulator does include a special VR mode, which you can access from the General Options menu, as shown in Figure 2-2. You can swap between desktop and VR mode at any time by pressing the key combination Ctrl+Tab on the keyboard, in case you experience any issues with your headset, or if you just need to show off something to your friends.

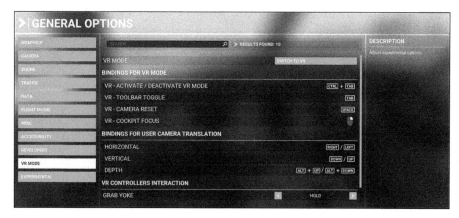

FIGURE 2-2:
Turn on VR mode from the General Options menu after launching Flight Simulator.

TIP

You must have a virtual reality headset in order to play Flight Simulator in VR mode. Any VR headset that can work in OpenXR should suffice, although Oculus and HTC headsets are quite popular at the time of this writing. See Chapter 4 for more information about choosing a headset.

After you turn on the headset and load up the game, enter VR mode from the General Options menu to get started. Because Flight Simulator is a simulation game, you can set up your joysticks, hands-on throttle-and-stick (HOTAS), or other control options to easily access them in VR. Consider having a set place for all your game accessories so that you can easily locate them in your play space.

# Running the Cockpit from the Keyboard

Playing Flight Simulator with a joystick or HOTAS adds to the immersive experience. However, not everyone has room for a massive custom setup, which is why the game comes with an easy-to-configure keyboard setup. Figure 2-3 shows Keyboard selected from the Controls Options menu. You find this menu by entering the Options menu from the main menu.

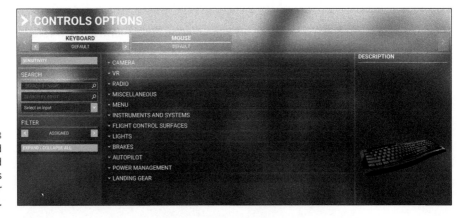

**FIGURE 2-3**
The keyboard puts a myriad of commands directly at your fingertips.

In the following sections, I present the various options that you can make use of during flight. For example, I show the keybinds for controlling essential parts of the aircraft, such as your instruments and flight control systems.

**REMEMBER**

Keep in mind that the default keybinds shown in this chapter aren't the only ones available. A large portion of the potential keybinds you can use in-game are unbound by default.

*Note:* In this chapter's tables, the arrow keys are simply referred to as *Up, Down, Right,* and *Left.* Any number key from the numpad has *Num* before the specific key (for example, *Num 1* means the 1 key on the numpad).

**TIP**

Remember that you can also access all of the key configuration information directly from the game by visiting the Options and Controls Options menu and then selecting Keyboard.

## Instruments and systems

Flight Simulator includes five main types of instruments and systems that you need to control within your aircraft. Each of these types comes with its own distinct set of keybinds as well. Table 2-1 groups the keybinds for each type of instrument and system.

**TABLE 2-1** **Keybinds for Instruments and Systems**

| Name | Keybind | Name | Keybind |
|---|---|---|---|
| **Anti-Ice** | | | |
| Toggle Anti-Ice | H | Toggle Pilot Heat | Shift+H |
| **Fuel System** | | | |
| Toggle Fuel Dump | Shift+Ctrl+D | Fuel Selector 1 Off | Ctrl+Alt+W |
| Fuel Selector 1 All | Alt+W | Toggle All Fuel Valves | Alt+V |
| **Flight Instruments** | | | |
| Select Airspeed Bug | Shift+Ctrl+R | Increase Heading Bug | Ctrl+Insert |
| Select Altitude Bug | Shift+Ctrl+Z | Select Heading Bug | Shift+Ctrl+H |
| Toggle Autorudder | Shift+Ctrl+U | Set Heading Indicator | D |
| Set Altimeter | B | Toggle Alternate Static | Alt+S |
| Decrease Heading Bug | Ctrl+Del | | |
| **Engine Instruments** | | | |
| Decrease Cowl Flap | Shift+Ctrl+C | Magnetos Both | Shift+Alt+F |
| Increase Cowl Flap | Shift+Ctrl+V | Magnetos Left | Shift+Alt+S |
| Select Engine | E | Magnetos Off | Shift+Alt+Q |
| Auto Start Engine | Ctrl+E | Magnetos Right | Shift+Alt+D |
| Engine Auto-Stop | Shift+Ctrl+E | Magnetos Start | Shift+Alt+G |
| Magneto | M | Toggle Master Ignition Switch | Alt+I |

*(continued)*

**TABLE 2-1** *(continued)*

| Name | Keybind | Name | Keybind |
|---|---|---|---|
| **Electrics** | | | |
| Toggle Master Alternator | Alt+A | Toggle Master Battery | Alt+B |
| Toggle Master Battery & Alternator | Shift+M | | |

# Cameras

Flight Simulator also comes with a slew of camera commands that you can take advantage of on a PC. And by the way, you find seven cameras, modes, and views that you can control. Table 2-2 shows off the keybinds for these camera controls.

**TABLE 2-2**     **Keybinds for Cameras and Views**

| Name | Keybind | Name | Keybind |
|---|---|---|---|
| **Cockpit Camera** | | | |
| Load Custom Camera 0–9 | Alt+# (for example, Alt+0 for camera 0) | Cockpit Quickview Up, Rear, Right, Left | Ctrl+Directional (Up, Down, Right, Left) |
| Load Next Custom Camera | K | Cockpit Quickview Cycle | Q |
| Load Previous Custom Camera | Shift+K | Reset Cockpit View | Ctrl+Spacebar or F |
| Save Custom Camera 0–9 | Ctrl+Alt+0-9 (for example, Ctrl+Alt+0 for camera 0) | Cockpit View Upper | Spacebar |
| Decrease Cockpit View Height | Down | Unzoom Cockpit View | Dash on the top row of the keyboard (-) |
| Increase Cockpit View Height | Up | Zoom Cockpit View | equal sign (=) |
| Translate Cockpit View Backward, Forward, Left, Right | Right Alt+Directional (Down, Up, Left, Right) | Toggle Smart Camera | S |
| Cockpit Look Down, Up, Left, Right | Shift+Directional (Down, Up, Left, Right) | | |

| Name | Keybind | Name | Keybind |
|------|---------|------|---------|
| **Drone Camera** | | | |
| Toggle Drone Depth of Field (DOF) | F1 | Lock Drone to Previous Target | Shift+T |
| Toggle Foreground Blur | F5 | Translate Drone Backward; Down; Forward; Left; Right; Up | S; F; W; A; D; R |
| Drone Top-Down View | Ctrl+Spacebar | Reset Drone Roll | Spacebar |
| Attach Drone to Next Target | Ctrl+Page Up | Reset Drone Target Offset | Num 5 |
| Attach Drone to Previous Target | Ctrl+Page Down | Roll Drone Right; Left | Num 9; Num 7 |
| Toggle Drone Auto Exposure; Auto Focus | Ctrl+F4; F4 | Pitch Drone Down; Up | Num 2; Num 8 |
| Decrease Drone Rotation Speed; Increase | F3; F4 | Yaw Drone Left; Right | Num 4; Num 6 |
| Decrease Drone Translation Speed; Increase | F1; F2 | Toggle Drone Follow Mode | Tab |
| Decrease Drone DOF; Increase Drone DOF | F2; F3 | Toggle Drone Lock Mode | Ctrl+Tab |
| Decrease Drone Exposure | Ctrl+F2 | Drone Zoom Increase | Num plus sign (+) |
| Increase Drone Exposure | Ctrl+F3 | Drone Zoom Decrease | Num minus sign (-) |
| Lock Drone to Next Target | T | Toggle Plane Controls | C |
| **External Camera** | | | |
| Reset External View | Ctrl+Spacebar or F | Unzoom External View | Dash on the top row of the keyboard (-) |
| External Quickview Left, Rear, Right, Top | Ctrl+Directional (Left, Down, Right, Up) | Zoom External View | equal sign (=) |
| **Fixed Camera** | | | |
| Toggle Fixed Camera 0–9 | Ctrl+Shift+# (for example, Ctrl+Shift+0 for camera 0) | Previous Fixed Camera | Shift+A |
| Reset Fixed Camera | F | Next Fixed Camera | A |

*(continued)*

**TABLE 2-2** *(continued)*

| Name | Keybind | Name | Keybind |
|------|---------|------|---------|
| **Instrument Views** | | | |
| Previous Instrument View | Shift+A | Unset Custom Smartcam Target | Shift+T |
| Next Instrument View | A | Next Smartcam Target | Page Up+Ctrl |
| Toggle Instrument View 0–9 | Ctrl+# (for example, Ctrl+0 for Instrument View 0) | Previous Smartcam Target | Page Down+Ctrl |
| Select Next POI (point of interest) | Page Up | Camera AI Player | Home+Ctrl |
| Reset Smartcam | Ctrl+F | Toggle Follow Smartcam Target | Page Down |
| Set Custom Smartcam Target | T | | |
| **Slew Mode** | | | |
| Slew Translate Up (Slow); (Fast) | F3; F4 | Slew Yaw Left; Right | Num 1; Num 3 |
| Slew Translate Backward; Forward | Num 2; Num 8 | Slew Pitch Down | Num 0 |
| Slew Translate Down (Fast); (Slow) | F1; A | Slew Pitch Down (Fast) | F8 |
| Slew Translate Left; Right | Num 4; Num 6 | Slew Pitch Up | 9 |
| Slew Y-Axis Translation Freeze | F2 | Slew Pitch Up (Fast); (Slow) | F5; F7 |
| Slew X-Axis Translation Freeze | Num 5 | Slew Pitch Freeze | F6 |
| Slew Roll Left; Right | Num 7; Num 9 | Toggle Slew Mode | Y |
| **Camera Mode Switches** | | | |
| Cockpit/External View Mode | End | Toggle Drone | Insert |

# Menu

You can use the Menu commands to quickly move around the game menu, to select important aspects of the mission, and more. Table 2-3 lists the keybinds for menu commands.

**TABLE 2-3**    **Keybinds for Menu Commands**

| Name | Keybind | Name | Keybind |
|------|---------|------|---------|
| Toggle Active Pause | Pause | Close Menu | Backspace |
| Toggle Pause | Esc | Fly | Enter |
| Toggle Basic Control Panel | Ctrl+C | Change Aircraft | F11 |
| Clear Search | Del | Liveries | F12 |
| Select 1; 2; 3; 4 | Alt+F1; Alt+F2; Alt+F3; Alt+F4 | See Specifications | F10 |
| Display Checklist | Shift+C | Help Menu | Tab |
| Next Toolbar Panel | period (.) | Restart Free Flight | Home |
| Previous Toolbar Panel | forward slash (/) | Restart Activity | Home |
| Back To Main Menu | End | | |

# Autopilot

Autopilot is a great feature that enables you to sit back and relax for a moment during your flight. These Autopilot commands (shown in Table 2-4) give control over to Autopilot quickly and easily.

**TABLE 2-4**    **Autopilot Keybinds**

| Name | Keybind | Name | Keybind |
|------|---------|------|---------|
| Autopilot Off | Shift+Alt+Z | Increase Autopilot Reference Airspeed | Shift+Ctrl+Insert |
| Autopilot On | Alt+Z | Decrease Autopilot Reference VS | Ctrl+End |
| Autopilot Airspeed Hold | Alt+R | Increase Autopilot Reference VS | Ctrl+Home |
| Decrease Autopilot Reference Altitude | Ctrl+Page Down | Toggle Autopilot Wing Leveler | Ctrl+V |
| Increase Autopilot Reference Altitude | Ctrl+Page Up | Arm Auto Throttle | Shift+R |
| Toggle Autopilot Hold for Approach; Attitude; Localizer; Mach | Ctrl+A; Ctrl+T; Ctrl+O; Ctrl+M | Auto Throttle To GA | Shift+Ctrl+G |
| Autopilot N1 Hold | Ctrl+S | Toggle Autopilot Master | Z |

*(continued)*

**TABLE 2-4** *(continued)*

| Name | Keybind | Name | Keybind |
|---|---|---|---|
| Autopilot Nav1 Hold | Ctrl+N | Toggle Avionics Master | Page Up |
| Decrease Autopilot N1 Reference | Ctrl+End | Toggle Flight Director | Ctrl+F |
| Increase Autopilot N1 Reference | Ctrl+Home | Toggle Yaw Damper | Ctrl+D |
| Decrease Autopilot Reference Airspeed | Shift+Ctrl+Del | | |

## Brakes

You use your brakes to slow down your aircraft while you're on the ground. Keep the keybinds in Table 2-5 handy for use while taxiing and landing on runways.

**TABLE 2-5** **Braking Keybinds**

| Name | Keybind | Name | Keybind |
|---|---|---|---|
| Brakes | Num Decimal (.) | Left Brake | Num Multiply (*) |
| Toggle Parking Brakes | Ctrl+Num Decimal (.) | Right Brake | Num Minus (-) |

## Power management

To manage your power during flight, you sometimes need to increase the mixture, as well as increase or decrease power to the propellers. Use the keybind commands listed in Table 2-6 to quickly make these changes.

## Flight control surfaces

The flight control surfaces keybinds include toggles and controls for your airplane's equipment, such as the flaps, the rudder, and the aileron. (You can get the lowdown on these pieces of equipment in Chapter 6.) You use these mechanical parts to run an aircraft smoothly, so make sure you know how to use the commands in Table 2-7 before taking off.

**TABLE 2-6**     **Power Management Keybinds**

| Name | Keybind | Name | Keybind |
|------|---------|------|---------|
| Mixture | | | |
| Decrease Mixture | Shift+Ctrl+F2 | Set Mixture Lean | Shift+Ctrl+F1 |
| Increase Mixture (Small) | Shift+Ctrl+F3 | Set Mixture Rich | Shift+Ctrl+F4 |
| Propeller | | | |
| Decrease Propeller Pitch | Ctrl+F2 | Increase Propeller Pitch | Ctrl+F3 |
| Propeller Pitch Hi | Ctrl+F4 | Propeller Pitch Lo | Ctrl+F1 |
| Throttle | | | |
| Decrease Throttle | F2 | Increase Throttle | F3 |
| Throttle Cut | F1 | | |

**TABLE 2-7**     **Flight Control Surface Keybinds**

| Name | Keybind | Name | Keybind |
|------|---------|------|---------|
| Primary Control Surfaces | | | |
| Aileron Left (Roll Left); Right (Roll Right) | Num 4; Num 6 | Toggle Water Rudder | Ctrl+W |
| Center Ailer Rudder | Num 5 | Rudder Left (Yaw Left); Right (Yaw Right) | Num 0; Enter |
| Elevator Down (Pitch Down); Up (Pitch Up) | Num 8; Num 2 | | |
| Secondary Control Surfaces | | | |
| Decrease Flaps; Increase Flaps | F6; F7 | Toggle Spoilers | Num Divide (/) |
| Extend Flaps; Retract Flaps | F8; F5 | | |
| Control Trimming Surfaces | | | |
| Aileron Trim Left; Right | Ctrl+Num 4; Ctrl+Num 6 | Rudder Trim Left; Right | Ctrl+Num 0; Ctrl+Enter |
| Elevator Trim Down (Nose Down); Up (Nose Up) | NUM 7; NUM 1 | | |

# Radio

You use the radio to keep in contact with air traffic control (ATC). The keybinds in Table 2-8 should help make communicating by radio a breeze.

TABLE 2-8    ## Radio Communications Keybinds

| Name | Keybind | Name | Keybind |
|------|---------|------|---------|
| **ADF/Comms** | | | |
| ADF | Shift+Ctrl+A | Com Radio | C |
| Set Com1 Standby | Shift+Ctrl+X | Com1 Switch To Standby | Alt+U |
| **DME and NAV** | | | |
| DME | F | | |
| Decrease NAV1 Frequency (Fract, Carry) | Shift+Ctrl+Page Down | Increase NAV1 Frequency (Fract, Carry) | Shift+Ctrl+Page Up |
| NAV1 Swap | Shift+Ctrl+N | NAV Radio | N |
| **VOR** | | | |
| Decrease VOR1 OBS | Shift+Ctrl+End | Increase VOR1 OBS | Shift+Ctrl+Home |
| VOR OBS | Shift+V | | |
| **XPNDR** | | | |
| Transponder | T | Set Transponder | Shift+Alt+W |
| Display ATC | Scroll Lock | ATC Panel Choice 0–9 | # (for example, 0 for panel 0) |
| Frequency Swap | X | Increase Wheel Speed | Shift |

# Lights

Lights come in handy for a multitude of flying activities — for example, for lighting the way when you're attempting a landing in the middle of the night. You can also toggle the interior lights on your aircraft to help you see around the cockpit more easily. Table 2-9 gives you the keybinds to use for all your lighting needs.

**TABLE 2-9**     **Lighting Keybinds**

| Name | Keybind | Name | Keybind |
|---|---|---|---|
| **Exterior Lights** | | | |
| Toggle Landing Lights | Ctrl+I | Landing Lights Down | Shift+Ctrl+Num 2 |
| Landing Lights Up | Shift+Ctrl+Num 8 | Landing Lights Home; Left; Right | Shift+Ctrl+Num 5 |
| Landing Lights Left | Shift+Ctrl+Num 4 | Landing Lights Right | Shift+Ctrl+Num 6 |
| Toggle Strobes | O | Toggle Beacon Light | Alt+H |
| Toggle Nav Light | Alt+N | Toggle Taxi Lights | Alt+J |
| **Interior Lights** | | | |
| Toggle Flashlight | Alt+I | Toggle Lights | I |

# Commanding the Cockpit with the Controller

If you'd prefer to use a controller to interface with Flight Simulator, rather than a keyboard (which we talk about in the section "Running the Cockpit from the Keyboard," earlier in this chapter), you can do just that. Although some players feel it's a bit less immersive to use a controller, it does provide a convenient and simple way to jump right into the action. However, keep in mind that when using a controller on the PC version of the game, you still need to use the keyboard for an exhaustive set of controls because your controller just doesn't have enough button combinations to match what you get with the keys of a full QWERTY keyboard.

**WARNING**

Because of the more limited button combinations on a controller (as compared to the keys on a keyboard), using a controller gives you a more condensed version of the options available to you in-game. If you want to tweak your experience further, you can always use a combination of keyboard and controller to heighten the realism factor in-game.

In the following tables (Table 10 through Table 13), I outline the various keybinds that you can use with a controller in Flight Simulator.

**TABLE 2-10**     # Cameras, Views, and Modes

| Name | Keybind | Name | Keybind |
|------|---------|------|---------|
| **Cockpit Camera** | | | |
| Previous Pilot Position | DPAD Down | Cockpit Look Down; Left; Right; Up | RS Down; RS Left; RS Right; RS Up |
| Next Pilot Position | DPAD Up | Cockpit Quickview Right; Left | DPAD Right; DPAD Left |
| Toggle Smart Camera | X | Reset Cockpit View | RS |
| **Drone Camera** | | | |
| Roll Drone Right; Left | RB; LB | Decrease Drone Rotation Speed | X+RB |
| Pitch Drone Up; Down | RS Up; RS Down | Increase Drone Rotation Speed | X+LB |
| Yaw Drone Left; Right | RS Left; RS Right | Decrease Drone Translation Speed | X+RT |
| Toggle Drone Follow Mode | RS | Increase Drone Translation Speed | X+LT |
| Toggle Drone Lock Mode | LS | Decrease Drone Depth of Field | B+LT |
| Increase Drone Zoom | Y+RT | Increase Drone Depth of Field | B+RT |
| Decrease Drone Zoom | Y+LT | Decrease Drone Exposure | Y+LB |
| Toggle Drone Depth of Field | B+Y | Increase Drone Exposure | Y+RB |
| Toggle Foreground Blur | B+DPAD Left | Translate Drone Backward; Down; Forward; Left; Right; Up | LS Down; LT; LS Up; LS Left; LS Right; RT |
| Drone Top-Down View | X+Y | Reset Drone Roll | RB+LB |
| Toggle Drone Auto Exposure | Y+LS | Reset Drone Target Offset | X+A |
| Toggle Drone Autofocus | B+LS | | |
| **External and Fixed Cameras** | | | |
| Reset External View | RS | External View Look Down; Left; Right | RS Down; RS Left; RS Right |
| Next Fixed Camera | DPAD Right | External Quickview Left; Rear; Right; Top | DPAD Right; DPAD Down; DPAD Left; DPAD Up |

| Name | Keybind | Name | Keybind |
|---|---|---|---|
| **Instrument Views** | | | |
| Previous Instrument View | DPAD Left | Next Instrument View | DPAD Right |
| **Slew Mode and Camera Mode Switches** | | | |
| Slew Translate Backward; Forward; Down; Up; Left; Right | LS Down; LS Up; LT; RT; LS Right; LS Left | Cockpit/External View Mode | Select |
| Slew Yaw Left; Right | RS Right; RS Left | Slew Pitch Down; Up | RS Up; RS Down |

**TABLE 2-11    In-Game Menu**

| Name | Keybind | Name | Keybind |
|---|---|---|---|
| Clear Search | Select | Liveries | Select |
| Toggle Pause | Start | See Specifications | Y |
| Back to Main Menu | Y | Help Menu | LS |
| Close Menu | B | Restart Free Flight | X |
| Fly | Start | Restart Activity | X |
| Change Aircraft | X | | |

**TABLE 2-12    Brake and Power Management Controls**

| Name | Keybind | Name | Keybind |
|---|---|---|---|
| **Brakes** | | | |
| Brakes | Y | Toggle Parking Brakes | Y+B |
| **Power Management** | | | |
| Decrease Throttle | B | Increase Throttle | A |

**TABLE 2-13**     **Flight Control Surfaces**

| Name | Keybind | Name | Keybinds |
|------|---------|------|----------|
| **Primary Control Surfaces** | | | |
| Ailerons Axis | LS Left/Right | Rudder Left (Yaw Left) | LT |
| Elevator Axis | LS Up/Down | Rudder Right (Yaw Right) | RT |
| **Secondary Control Surfaces** | | | |
| Decrease Flaps | LB | Increase Flaps | RB |
| **Control Trimming Surfaces** | | | |
| Rudder Trim Left | Y+DPAD Left | Elevator Trim Down (Nose Down) | Y+DPAD Up |
| Rudder Trim Right | Y+DPAD Right | Elevator Trim Up (Nose Up) | Y+DPAD Down |

# Chapter **3**

# Heading to Flight School

E veryone knows the most exciting part of a brand-new game is finally sitting down to play it. If you're ready to jump into Flight Simulator, it's time to enroll in flight school, so to speak. After you take this chapter's detailed tour of the game's Main Menu, World Map, and various other options, you can finally jump in and see what it feels like to climb into the cockpit of a real-life (or real-virtual) aircraft.

You can also find beginner's tips suitable for future ace pilots — which means you, of course. Just because you have a lot of new information to digest doesn't mean that you can't transform into an expert pilot in due time. With a bit of practice, you might soon find yourself explaining some of these mechanics to another new player. Sometimes, things really do come full circle like that.

This chapter helps you get ready to embark on your first real (virtual) flight — after you prep with important reading, terms, tips, and tutorials. Soon enough, preflight tasks become second nature. For now, if you're reading this chapter, just relax, absorb, and get ready to fly.

## Exploring the Game's Main Menu

Welcome to Flight Simulator, Pilot-in-Training! You may find Flight Simulator a bit daunting on your first launch. Right off the bat, you have so much to see and do, with plenty of options to tweak your experience, as well as predetermined routes to explore, tutorials to help you figure things out, and other ways to interact with the game. All the features become old hat at some point, but coming into the game for the first time is a little like walking into a mall crowded with dozens of stores: You may struggle to figure out exactly where to start.

Before you can leave the ground, you should know a few important things about settling in for your first flight. Whether this is the first time you've ever seen the Flight Simulator interface — or you want to get a bit more in-depth information about how to use it — this section helps get your first flight experience underway (even if you're afraid of heights).

## Noting the tabs on the Main Menu

When you first load Flight Simulator, you face the Main Menu, which is split into multiple sections. I number these sections for you and show them in Figure 3-1. The Main Menu is your main port of call in the game (as the title suggests), and it offers the sections shown in Table 3-1.

You can find tabs along the top margin of the Main Menu screen. Pay attention to these tabs, which give you access to the welcome screen, profile information, and game options.

Here's a quick look at the tabs and their features:

>> **Welcome:** This is the main tab, where you land when you first load the game. From here, you can choose from Discovery Flight, World Map, Flight Training, Activities, and the Marketplace to get started playing.

>> **Profile:** The tab you select to view your Pilot Profile, Hangar, and Logbook. You can also manage any additional content on your account here by using the Content Manager.

>> **Options:** The tab you select to access and adjust all the various options in Flight Simulator. Check out Chapters 10 and 12 for more information about the options for aircraft, departure and arrival airports, weather conditions, and other aspects of your virtual flights.

## Taking the Discovery Flights

Embark on stunning flights to landmarks around the world or choose to play training scenarios to get up to speed on Flight Simulator controls by jumping right in. Entering Discovery Flights mode enables you to recreate famous movie moments or visit locations around the world that are on your bucket list.

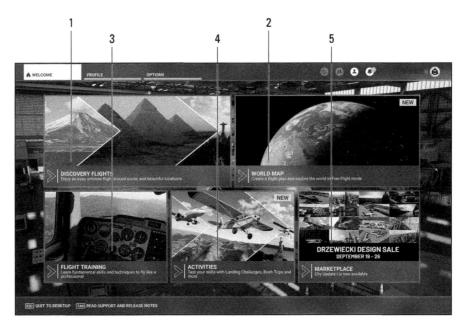

**FIGURE 3-1:**
The Main
Menu in Flight
Simulator,
with sections
numbered.

**TABLE 3-1**  **Main Menu Sections**

| Section | Name | What You Find There |
|---------|------|---------------------|
| 1 | Discovery Flights | Predetermined flight paths and specifications |
| 2 | World Map | A representation of Earth as a globe, including options for flight specifications |
| 3 | Flight Training | A two-hour training session on basic controls and maneuvers |
| 4 | Activities | Preset flights that offer a specific flight challenge or exploration goal |
| 5 | Marketplace | Additional content for purchase and download |

Each section of the Discovery Flights menu offers predetermined locations that you can choose from and fly to, which can help new players get started. Taking these built-in flights can help eliminate some of the choice paralysis that comes along with trying to choose specifications for your first flight.

Entering this segment of the menu for the first time gives you the opportunity to fly to six locations around the world:

>> **Mount Everest (Nepal):** See the tallest mountain in the world and try not to crash into it.

>> **Giza (Egypt):** Get an aerial view of the Great Pyramids.

- **Bora Bora (French Polynesia):** Acquaint yourself with the shores of this tropical paradise.

- **Naples (Italy):** Drink in the culture of one of the oldest continually occupied cities in the world.

- **New York City (USA):** Bop around the Big Apple and get to know the city that never sleeps.

- **Rio de Janeiro (Brazil):** Visit the country's second largest city and view the legendary Christ the Redeemer statue.

Flight Simulator removes all the guesswork from these self-contained flight experiences. Everything — from the type of aircraft you fly to the points of interest and cities in the area that you're flying to — is carefully selected for you. Follow these simple steps to take a preset Discovery Flight:

1. **Select a destination that you want to fly to from the Discovery Flights menu.**

   The preflight screen appears, giving you an explanation of what your selected flight entails, including details such as starting altitude, aircraft model, and a brief description of the area.

2. **When you're ready to experience your exciting mission, click the Fly option in the lower right corner of the screen.**

   You can embark on your Discovery Flight immediately.

## Searching on the World Map

The Flight Simulator World Map is the main hub where you inevitably spend a lot of your playing time. You can search the entire globe from this map for places of interest, choose one, and fly there. But before you indulge in a flight, take the time to investigate the important terms and variety of options available from this section of the game.

**TIP**

To make the most of the World Map, become familiar with the codes used to identify airports. An *International Civil Aviation Organization (ICAO) code* is the (usually) four-letter code that designates airports around the world. Pilots and air traffic controllers use these codes in communication. An *International Air Transport Associate (IATA) code,* also known as a station code or location identifier, is a three-character code for airports around the world. Almost every airport has an ICAO code, but typically, only airports that host airlines have an IATA code.

The main difference between these two codes is related to the organization involved; the ICAO is a UN-based, inter-governmental organization whereas the IATA is a trade organization. You hear about IATA codes so much (in the U.S.) because that code is typically also the airport's FAA ID.

Check out Figure 3-2 and Table 3-2 for a look at the many features of the Flight Simulator World Map.

**TABLE 3-2:    Sections of the World Map**

| Section | Name | What You Do There |
|---------|------|-------------------|
| A | Aircraft Selection | Select the aircraft that you want to fly. |
| B | From Selection | Choose the airport from which you want to depart by typing in an airport name, city, or ICAO or IATA code. |
| C | To Selection | Choose the airport at which you want to arrive by typing in an airport name, city, or ICAO or IATA code. |
| D | Flight Conditions | Set special flight options, such as whether you want to turn on live weather options (discussed in further detail in Chapter 13) and whether you're going to want to set up a multiplayer session. |
| E | Time of Day | Choose this option to change the time of day for your flight. Move the slider to the left and right to watch the Earth rotate so that you can get an idea of the type of lighting you can get when you're soaring through the skies. |
| F | Fly Now | This yellow button lights up when everything is ready for you to start your flight. Click this button to begin your flight session whenever you have everything set to your liking. |
| G | Search bar | Type anything you want to search for in this bar, either by using the onscreen keyboard or a physical keyboard. You can search for airports by their ICAO/IATA codes, cities and landmarks, and even global coordinates. |

If you know the custom GPS coordinates of a location on Earth that you want to visit, you can type them into the World Map Search bar to set up a custom location to fly to.

## Engaging in Flight Training

Flight Simulator's Flight Training feature is an integral part of figuring out how to fly your plane. It's a two-hour training session that you can take part in before you ever set foot inside a (virtual) cockpit. Take the time to go through this Flight Simulator experience, especially if you've never played the game before. Flight Training gives you a great chance to get acquainted with all the game's controls and find out what climbing into a plane feels like before you ever start up the craft.

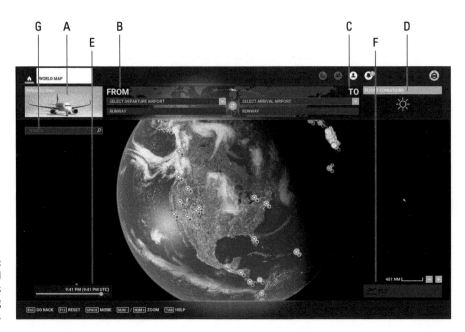

FIGURE 3-2:
The World
Map offers
you exciting
options.

When you open the Flight Training menu, a few different categories appear onscreen to choose from, all of which can help you get ready to hit the air. Special voiceovers during instruction help you figure out what to do, too, so you aren't left totally to your own devices.

Here's a description of the main Flight Training sessions:

>> **Basic Controls (eight modules):** Take a look at this training session to find out more about the basics of handling your aircraft, as well as all the ways you can control it, whether you're using a keyboard and mouse, game pad, or flight stick.

>> **Takeoff and Landing (six modules):** In this training session, find out how to take off in your aircraft, as well as how to land without, well, going down in flames. Definitely something important to know.

>> **VFR Navigation (five modules):** This training session is all about Visual Flight Rules (VFR), as well as how you can use landmarks to fly the friendly skies.

>> **Airline Training (two modules):** This training session gives you some (virtual) real-world experience by way of putting you in the pilot's seat of an Airbus A320neo and letting you take to the sky.

After you complete each training session, you get a score, as well as a grade. You can always attempt each segment again to try for a better score. If you're just starting out, practice makes you more ready for anything that comes your way.

# Adding flight challenges by using Activities

The Activities menu selection enables you choose a few different missions in which you can take on challenges or explore the globe. When you go into this menu option, here's what you find:

>> **Landing Challenges:** You get 24 different landing challenges to explore, each with their own unique aspects:

- *Dangerous Airports:* Some of the more difficult airports to navigate for landing.

- *Famous Airports:* Some of the larger airports across the globe.

- *Higher Winds:* High winds make it difficult to land because you have to contend with opposing forces from these strong winds that can push your plane off course — in addition to all the usual challenges about a landing. High winds can spell disaster for anyone who isn't a pro.

>> **Bush Trips:** Don't really feel like jumping into a challenge? No problem. Try out a Bush Trip instead, which lets you take a cross-country journey that includes a full navigation itinerary. You just need to turn off your brain (somewhat, at least) and fly. By flying a Bush Trip, you can focus less on staying in the air and more on all the unique sights on the ground below you.

# Scoping out the Marketplace

The Marketplace is exactly what it sounds like. You can go here to buy and download additional content for Flight Simulator. You can find a variety of products to purchase, including additional aircrafts, *liveries* (color, graphic, and typographical treatments) to decorate your aircrafts, airports, optional missions to complete, and scenery (such as night versions of locations) to help enhance your game's World Map. You might find an occasional free download in the Marketplace, but most are paid add-ons that you need to buy with real money.

New Marketplace additions are always sorted by date so that you can quickly find the latest products for purchase. Most of this content is not created by developer Asobo Studios, but instead by third-party creators who are approved to submit content for Flight Simulator.

After you pay for your new content, it becomes available immediately and installs automatically after download. You don't need to perform any additional steps to use it in-game.

# Early Flight Tips for Future Ace Pilots

After you familiarize yourself with Flight Simulator's menus and options (which you can do by flipping back to the section "Exploring the Game's Main Menu," earlier in this chapter), here are a couple of tips to keep in mind before you start playing — or as I like to say, before you set off on your journey to become an ace pilot:

>> **Plan for 30 minutes to an hour of flight time for one short flight per session.** From configuring your flight to choosing your aircraft and arriving at your destination, a flight session in Flight Simulator probably takes at least 30 minutes (depending on your destination). You don't want to be interrupted during this time, otherwise, you may find that your craft crashes and burns — and no one wants that, obviously.

If you're staying local, 30 minutes to an hour should be enough time allotted for a shorter flight. But if you plan on going cross-country or on longer flights, you may need a few hours, so plan your real-life schedule accordingly. For a short time, you're going to be a real pilot in-game, after all.

>> **Start off with the Easy difficulty setting to get your bearings in the cockpit.** For your first few flights, it's well worth the effort to change the game's difficulty settings. To do so, head into the Assistance menu and adjust each individual aspect of a flight — from Piloting and Aircraft Systems, to Failure & Damage, to Notifications. Change each setting to Easy to help facilitate your first flights.

REMEMBER

The easier (and less realistic) your flight's options, the less difficulty you have completing the flight. You can change the difficulty settings for each flight aspect at any time during your flight, even if you're already in the air, by using the in-game menu and choosing Support.

>> **Choose a simple plane to fly first.** Selecting a plane that's both stable and simple to control can almost guarantee that you have a great first flight. For easy flying, choose a Cessna model as your fledgling flyer. Choosing a plane from the Cessna line of aircrafts tends to provide a much more stable option than larger airplanes with multiple engines, which makes keeping it in the air simpler to manage.

TIP

The Cessna 172 Skyhawk is a particularly great aircraft because it features realistic autopilot capabilities, as well as an attractive exterior. Practice with a Cessna enough that you feel confident flying a simpler type of plane before you make the jump to jets or other larger aircraft later on.

# Playing Those Tutorials

After you delve into Flight Simulator 2020 and see everything the game has waiting for you (which I go over in the section "Exploring the Game's Main Menu," earlier in this chapter), you may feel tempted to jump in and start doing whatever it is that you want to do. With all kinds of different aircrafts at your disposal and airports to visit, who wouldn't want to jump into a cockpit before reading the manual, so to speak? Definitely don't go that route with Flight Simulator because learning the fundamentals is essential to gaining confidence in the virtual air. Instead, absolutely play the lengthy tutorials that you can find in the Flight Training segment, as described in the section "Engaging in Flight Training," earlier in this chapter.

The game has carefully crafted these tutorials to help you get started without having too much frustration. And although I hope this book gives you all the assistance you need to feel comfortable flying the friendly skies, these tutorials are also extremely important in helping you figure out how to play the game. I highly recommend that you play the tutorials because they provide hands-on time in a controlled setting. Even if you decide to use only this book as a companion to what's in store in the game, the tutorials give you the basic skills that are essential for every flight.

# Taking off the Training Wheels and Engaging the Landing Wheels

There comes a time in every aspiring pilot's life where you need to take off the training wheels — or, in this case, engage the landing wheels. You can prepare extensively for your first real hands-on simulated flight as long as you want, but eventually you need to jump in and get your feet wet. But you don't need to feel nervous or scared.

For one thing, you have the luxury of flying a digital aircraft on your side. No one's going to get hurt if you don't get it right the first time. Furthermore, if you make a mistake, you can correct things by doing something as easy as restarting your flight or quitting for a while and coming back with fresh eyes. Whatever your approach to figuring out Flight Simulator and becoming the best pilot you can be, the following sections give you some of the basics.

# Preparing for takeoff

If you want to get an aircraft into the air, you need to master the art of the takeoff. Each plane you pilot has its own set of unique features, but every single craft is beholden to the same physics and principles of flight as the rest of the planes you find in the game.

REMEMBER

Each time you prepare for takeoff, you essentially perform the same steps over and over. You can't just suss out the procedure by pulling levers and pressing buttons, though. You need to take a very specific set of actions if you want to make it into the air. Although I still recommend that you follow the in-game tutorial to figure out additional flight preparation steps that may apply to certain planes, the following sections offer a one-size-fits-all overview that gets you into the air and flying around in no time at all.

## Making adjustments before takeoff

After you load Flight Simulator (which you can read the procedure for in Chapter 1) and choose your plane (discussed in Chapter 12), the game is ready to go, just like you are. Your plane is on the runway, and that stretch of pavement before you is calling your name. Time to start moving, right? Not so fast. Before you move even an inch down the runway, an air traffic controller (ATC) needs to clear you for takeoff.

In some tutorials (or if you choose to ignore the ATC clearing requirement), you can leave this detail to your virtual copilot. You can find this clearance requirement toggle (on and off) in the Flight Assistance settings. In a tutorial or with the AI Radio Communications toggle on, your copilot handles any conversations you need to have with the ATC.

After you receive permission from the ATC to take off, follow these steps before hitting the throttle:

1. **Press the B button on the keyboard to set your altimeter automatically.**

   In most cases, the altimeter will be set to 29.92, which is the standard altimeter reading.

   REMEMBER

   An *altimeter* is a device that measures altitude above sea level. Most altimeters are barometric, which means that they measure altitude by calculating the location's air pressure.

2. **Press the F7 key on the top row of your keyboard or up and down on the controller D-pad to set your flaps.**

   Find out more about flaps and their functions (and other successful start-up details) in Chapter 8.

3. **Check that the trimmer wheel on your aircraft is set to the TO (takeoff) position.**

4. **Set your fuel mixture lever on your aircraft to 100%.**

5. **Release your aircraft's parking brake by pushing it inward.**

   You can find the parking brake in a similar location to where you can usually find an automobile's hood release switch.

   Alternatively, you can simply press Ctrl+Del or left on the controller D-pad to disengage the brake.

## Getting off the ground correctly

After you finish your preflight routine (see the preceding section), it's time for takeoff. If you need a quick boost of confidence, don't worry. You've got this! You're about to do something very, very cool — and after you get the important preflight actions down and committed to memory (you definitely will at some point), you can look back on this moment fondly as the beginning of a long and fruitful journey as a talented pilot.

We're about to take your chosen aircraft into the sky and keep it there, at least for a short while. When you're ready to takeoff, follow these steps:

1. **Check your aircraft's position on the runway by using the Flight Simulator camera.**

   To ensure that your (and your aircraft's) nose is centered on the runway, position the camera a bit higher than the plane itself. With this camera position, you have a better view of where the plane actually is and can fine-tune your plane's location and movements through your game's input device.

2. **Move the throttle lever to 100%, which represents full throttle speed.**

   Make this move by using gentle motions, such as moving the mouse upward slowly and smoothly, or pressing the F3 button.

**WARNING**

   Don't adjust the throttle by using a hasty, jerking movement, and don't throw the plane into high gear like you would a car in the middle of a drag race. Doing so can lead you to stall or overspeed the plane.

   After you achieve full throttle speed, your RPM clock raises. Your plane starts moving — but don't panic.

3. **While your plane is moving, make correcting adjustments via the triggers on your gamepad or your keyboard to ensure that you keep the craft centered on the runway.**

If your plane isn't moving in a perfectly straight line down the runway, correct this positioning immediately so you don't run off the pavement. To counteract the pull in a certain direction (away from center), you can pull on your rudder in the opposite direction. At this point, you want to be moving at a pretty slow clip down the runway, as close to the middle as you can get.

**TIP**

If keeping the aircraft moving straight down the runway is difficult for you, you can activate an option to have this controlled movement completed for you by the game's copilot (via Rudder Assist). Discover the game's many assists and other accessibility options in Chapter 6.

4. **Keep an eye on your speed (on your plane's dashboard), and when you achieve 50 to 60 knots, pull back on the stick (via your yoke, joystick, or keyboard) to actuate the elevators.**

   Your plane begins to leave the ground. Like with the throttle in Step 2, don't use hasty or jerky motions. Be extremely gentle and deliberate with your actions in this step and be patient. Your craft moves slowly but surely upward into the air, as long as you continue to maintain the same amount of pressure on the elevators and don't overdo it by pulling back as hard as possible. At these lower speeds, if your climb is too aggressive, you'll stall.

After you eventually reach cruising altitude, flying is as simple as maintaining the same speed and altitude in the air. Congratulations, you made it!

## Practicing safe landings

As you know, what goes up must eventually come down. After you're satisfied with exploring the air and trying everything you can accomplish (such as flying over your hometown) while you're up there, you can look forward to making a smooth landing. Choose an airport and a runway to head back to (even the one from which you took off). (Be sure to check out Chapter 19 for a few destinations that you may want to visit.)

When you get close to the airport where you plan to land and receive ATC clearance for landing, follow these steps:

1. **Position your aircraft as close to the center of the runway as possible and dial back on the throttle (by pressing F2 on the top row of the keyboard or B on a controller., for example) to slow the plane down.**

   Keep an eye on your speed and aim to get below 80 knots in an effort to get as close to the runway as possible for a smooth landing.

You may also need to experiment with pitching your plane's nose in an upward direction (by positioning the yoke or joystick) to avoid hitting the ground. You don't want to crash this close to completing your flight, after all.

Eventually, you find yourself (and your aircraft) hovering over the runway. You're almost home free now!

2. **Cut back on the throttle to let the plane get into more of a gliding pattern (check out Chapter 9 for more on the glide for landing) while you descend even closer to the runway.**

REMEMBER

Keep the plane's nose a bit higher in the air and look downward — but do it all with gentle pushes and care. Take as long as you can to dip onto the runway, which gives you and your virtual passengers (when you have them) the smoothest possible landing experience.

3. **After your aircraft touches the ground, finish the landing by reducing throttle to a taxi speed of 20 knots and taxiing to the gate or hangar.**

Use the rudder controls to direct your aircraft to the correct arrival location.

Chapter **4**

# Virtual Planes, Real Pilot: Flight Simulator in VR

*irtual reality* (VR), a simulated experience that can mimic or completely alter an experience in the real world, can enhance just about any gaming event you can think of, whether that's spending carefree days fishing in a virtual stream or playing a round of virtual mini golf with your friends. Similarly, adding a VR headset into the mix while using Microsoft Flight Simulator 2020 transforms it into a much more immersive game. You transform from an amateur pilot who's viewing a TV or computer screen into a pilot who's occupying the cockpit for real (or, at least, as real as you can feel when you're not actually in a cockpit).

Flight Simulator's virtual reality support can make the entire game feel totally different — more realistic and engrossing. If you want to make the experience feel like you're actually seated in the cockpit of the plane you choose, virtual reality is undoubtedly your next stop. Getting your equipment and settings just right when preparing for your first VR outing can be tricky, but this chapter can help you make sure you get everything dialed in, whether you're taking off for the first time or the fiftieth.

In this chapter, I show you the ins and outs of playing in VR and what you need to have the best experience possible. After you spend a few hours soaring through the sky in virtual reality — with the ability to look around your cabin in the plane of your choice — I predict that you'll never want to go back to traditional flight sim gameplay again. Get ready for a literal game-changer, and one of the best things about modern gaming: making you feel like you're actually there in virtual reality.

# Experiencing a Whole New (Virtual) World

Flight Simulator is a thrill ride like no other from the moment you choose your favorite plane and get ready for takeoff. But the experience becomes truly extraordinary and jaw-dropping when you're in virtual reality. The game's immersion factor expands tenfold because you may as well have, for all intents and purposes, jumped into the world on your headset.

REMEMBER

When you add VR capability to Flight Simulator, instead of sitting on your sofa or in your desk chair, you feel the virtual experience of being the pilot in the cabin. You can look around the plane's interior, out onto the horizon, or down at the controls in front of you and feel like you're actually in the cockpit, about to head off on a cross-country flight.

The good news? If you find that you totally love Flight Simulator in VR and, in fact, prefer to play while fully immersed in virtual reality, you can do that for the foreseeable future. But the first step on this journey is putting your foot forward into the world of VR — evaluating the pluses and the minuses.

## Going for the enhanced experience of VR play

Implementing virtual reality play in Flight Simulator changes the experience in significant ways, including your

>> **Perception of the virtual aircraft:** Instead of being limited to the ways you can adjust the in-game camera to look around, you can look around with your VR headset as if you're really inside the plane. Figure 4-1 shows how the cockpit looks in a VR flight. With this enhanced perception, you can truly interact with your environment and simply look at what you want to touch without having to constantly adjust the camera. (Chapter 2 offers a look at the keys and buttons needed to adjust cameras from the keyboard or controller.)

>> **Experience with aircraft controls:** You can reach out and tweak your plane settings and get into your takeoff and landing sequences (check out Chapter 3) by way of actually turning knobs and pressing buttons with your controllers. It's an extremely visceral, hands-on experience.

TIP

Take time to carefully consider whether the virtual reality mode of play is something you're willing to implement. It's a cool way to see a vibrant picture of taking a plane up into the air, but it may not fit the budget or resources for everyone. The following sections explain why implementing VR in Flight Simulator takes commitment.

## Considering the potential downsides

Virtual reality is still very much a mode of play that's in its infancy, in comparison to the default video game play that most people recognize. And so, VR equipment isn't as widely adopted as, say, consoles and handheld gaming platforms. And although you may really enjoy looking around you to take in your surroundings through your VR headset, you need to take some things into consideration before you adopt VR. Consider these aspects before committing:

>> **Extra expense:** VR hardware isn't the cheapest gaming hardware you can purchase at the moment. And for this particular game (Flight Simulator), to play it in VR at all, you must have a decently powered PC, which can also get pricey, as well as a corresponding virtual reality headset.

   All of these things can begin to add up when you consider costs because they're all purchases that you must make in addition to buying the Flight Simulator software. The following section and the section "Appraising Hearty Headsets," later in this chapter, give you an idea of the equipment specifications and costs required for VR.

>> **Setup and usability factors:** A VR headset can take a while to get set up and working properly, especially if you've never used one before. Some of the situations you run in to may require that you

- *Account for wearing eyeglasses.* Glasses can interfere with the fit of the headset. In this case, you can purchase a spacer so that the headset fits better on your face (if your headset doesn't come with one.) Alternatively, you can purchase prescription lenses for your headset which is more comfortable, but also more expensive.

- *Deal with said eyeglasses that fog up.* You may have to deal with fogging if your headset isn't properly ventilated. You can remedy this by purchasing anti-fogging spray and applying it to your glasses.

- *Figure out how to orient yourself.* You need to make a link between the real world and the virtual one. To make this link, you can set a boundary with your headset that you can always see in-game.

REMEMBER

Regardless of the pricier equipment and potential setup hassle, VR gaming in Flight Simulator makes every flight feel much more real. And you can't say that about every single gaming experience you have, after all. I believe that every fan of Flight Simulator should find a way to give VR play a try. If you don't have your own VR equipment, perhaps you have friends who can let you give their VR game a test flight.

## Curbing motion sickness

You may find yourself susceptible to motion sickness while gaming, especially if you've never played a virtual reality game before. VR-induced motion sickness can be debilitating, and it can keep you from enjoying the game at all if you're constantly feeling nauseous or dizzy.

Ways to deal with motion sickness include taking frequent breaks and avoiding any flying acrobatics as you acclimate to VR play. Set time aside to completely step away from the game so that you can look away from the screen. Drink plenty of fluids. Take a walk outside and get some fresh air; both actions can help eliminate potential queasiness. Then you can jump back in and start flying again with minimal interruptions.

# Preparing for VR Gaming

When you want the unique opportunity of flying around the world in a craft of your choosing in virtual reality, you're no doubt champing at the bit to get going, right? But first, you need to attend to a few details before you can scramble into the cockpit and visit the seven wonders of the modern world. So hold your horses a bit and be smart about VR preparation.

Before you ever take a VR flight, you need to check a few settings and specifications to see whether your setup can take on the world of virtual reality. Unfortunately, you can't just download the game, plug in the headset, and take your VR flight. That easy sequence comes later, to be sure, but your first adventure requires a bit more planning and finesse.

Anyone who wants to get started with VR in Flight Simulator needs to address the following equipment needs before taking flight:

» **Assessing computing equipment for proper power:** See the following section for the necessary computer specifications.

» **Choosing the right VR headset and associated controllers:** Find recommendations in the section "Appraising Hearty Headsets," later in this chapter.

» **Getting the settings and performance options in Flight Simulator just right:** Check out the section "Tweaking Game Performance Settings," later in this chapter, for specifics.

## Verifying the potency of computing equipment

First and foremost, to implement VR in Flight Simulator, you need PC power to sustain what can be an extremely resource-heavy application. If you have a gaming PC that can run most of today's resource-dependent games (or if you're already running Flight Simulator without any big issues), you're already part of the way to achieving the right computing platform. You're going to need a decently powerful PC to make sure that it can handle both the Flight Simulator game and the stress that VR adds to the normal performance requirements.

Table 4-1 outlines the minimum and recommended specifications for a PC that can run Flight Simulator in VR mode, as provided by Microsoft.

## Targeting the other gaming hardware you need

You must have a VR headset and associated controllers to enjoy Flight Simulator in VR mode. You can choose from a variety of headset options at a variety of price points. Figure 4-2 shows a few of the possible VR headsets that you might want to try.

**TABLE 4-1**  **PC Specifications for Flight Simulator in VR Mode**

| Specification | Minimum | Recommended |
|---|---|---|
| OS | Windows 10 (November 2019 Update — 1909) | Windows 10 (November 2019 Update — 1909) |
| DirectX | DirectX 11 | DirectX 11 |
| CPU | Intel i5-8400 or equivalent | i9-9900K or equivalent |
| GPU | Nvidia GTX 1080 or equivalent | Nvidia RTX 2080 Ti or equivalent |
| VRAM | 8GB | 11GB |
| RAM | 16GB | 32GB |
| HDD | 150GB | 150GB |
| Bandwidth | 5 Mbps | 20 Mbps |

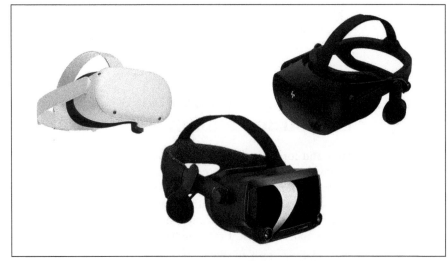

**FIGURE 4-2:** Some of the headsets you can choose from for your first VR flight.

Courtesy of Meta, HP INDIA SALES PRIVATE LIMITED, Valve Corporation

The section "Appraising Hearty Headsets," later in this chapter, gives you great information for evaluating which headset to buy, so be sure to consult that section before locking in a purchase. Even if you have no idea what kind of headset to look for or what you might need to do if you start feeling queasy when you strap it on, that section has you covered.

## Prepping your game settings for VR play

After you check off the physical and technical requirements for VR play — you have a PC that's powerful enough, as well as an appropriate VR headset and controllers — the remaining preparation involves setting up the Flight Simulator game itself for VR play.

So, you have to ask yourself the question: Are you prepared to deal with the somewhat challenging technical tweaks and specifications required to get into the world of virtual reality?

REMEMBER

If you don't like to spend time tweaking and setting up additional modes of a game that you can enjoy already without doing so, then playing in VR may not be for you. If you don't mind the extra effort and feel that you're somewhat technically inclined, get ready to jump in with both feet. Check out the section "Tweaking Game Performance Settings," later in this chapter, which leads you through the menus and performance settings that affect the quality of the VR experience in Flight Simulator.

# Appraising Hearty Headsets

Everyone who wants to dabble in the world of virtual reality needs to buy hardware in order to do so. You don't live in the far-off future where you can just turn on a game and enjoy it like it's a hologram floating in the air in front of you. You need hardware — the headset apparatus and associated controllers — to help you interface with your favorite VR games.

To cut down on the frustration of comparison shopping, I offer information on exceptional hardware choices for three types of budgets. So whether you want to splurge, add just a bit of oomph to your setup, or save the most money you can on your equipment, you're covered. Table 4-2 gives a quick-and-dirty look at the three hardware options, and in the following sections, I give some details about each one.

TIP

You might want to grab a pen and some paper to take notes from the following sections for your upcoming shopping trip!

| TABLE 4-2 | | Suggested Headset Options | |
|---|---|---|---|
| Brand and Model | Cost | Pros | Cons |
| Meta (Oculus) Quest 2 | $399 | Lower cost; three-hour play time per charge. Can be used wire-free. | Requires a cable link to be completely reliable. Lower specs than other headsets. |
| HP Reverb G2 | $599 | High resolution; adjustable field of vision | Not outstanding controllers |
| Valve Index | $999 | High resolution; comfort and adjustability | High cost |

## Meta Quest 2: The low-budget pick

The Meta (formerly Oculus) Quest 2 is a fantastic and budget-friendly option for players not looking to spend too much cash on flying in VR mode in Flight Simulator. The headset itself is, by far, the best for entry-level players in general VR applications, as well as fledgling flyers. Figure 4-3 shows the Meta Quest 2 and its cable.

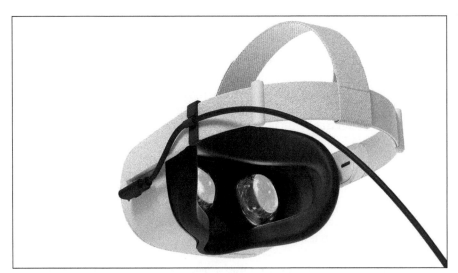

FIGURE 4-3:
The Meta Quest 2, pictured alongside the Quest 2 Link cable.

*Courtesy of Meta*

Here's what the Meta Quest 2 has to offer:

>> A Snapdragon XR2 processor with 6GB of RAM and up to 256GB of storage attached to the headset itself

>> An LCD display with 1232-x-1920 resolution per eye

>> A built-in battery that can give you two to three hours a charge, depending on how regularly you use it

However, the Meta Quest 2 is a wireless headset that isn't compatible with Flight Simulator right out of the box. The headset hardware doesn't have the power to work with a resource-heavy game without the addition of a powerful gaming computer to back it up. As a result, you also need to buy the Meta Link, which is an additional USB-C cable that you need so that you can attach your Quest 2 to your PC (so much for wireless!).

Connecting the headset adds enough power to play games across both Oculus and Steam titles (such as Half-Life: Alyx), in addition to VR in Flight Simulator.

REMEMBER

Keep in mind that you also need a Facebook account if you purchase a Meta Quest 2 because an account is required to log into and operate the device.

## HP Reverb G2: The affordable upgrade pick

If you want a higher-quality VR experience that's all about excellent resolution (without having to purchase an additional cable), the HP Reverb G2, shown in Figure 4-4, is your best option. It's a couple of hundred dollars more than the budget Meta Quest 2 (see the preceding section), but it's well worth the upgrade.

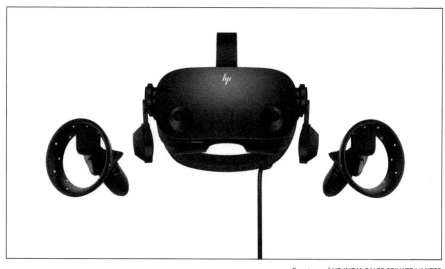

FIGURE 4-4:
The HP
Reverb G2
virtual reality
headset.

*Courtesy of HP INDIA SALES PRIVATE LIMITED*

The HP Reverb G2 comes with these features:

>> Two 2.89-inch LCD displays with a resolution of 2160 x 2160, for a combined 4320-x-2160 resolution

>> Manual adjustments that you can make to the headset itself, giving you better field of vision (FOV) and better controller tracking than what the Meta Quest 2 can provide

>> Great sound provided by the built-in headphones

>> Comfortable straps for longtime wear that won't drag you down

Although the HP Reverb G2 requires a powerful PC to run, it provides, by far, one of the best visual experiences you can find for Flight Simulator, and it won't break the bank. Although the associated controllers aren't the best on the market, the device is still very much worth the purchase price.

## Valve Index: The splurge pick

If you don't mind spending a bit more money on your Flight Simulator experience, the Valve Index is undoubtedly for you. As of this writing, it's the best headset hardware that the world of VR can provide — and its price does reflect that. But if you want the most realistic flights that you can find in the realm of flight simulators, this is the headset to trust. Figure 4-5 shows the Valve Index in all its glory.

**FIGURE 4-5:**
The Valve
Index.

*Courtesy of Valve Corporation*

The Valve Index features

>> Dual 3.5-inch LCD displays with a resolution of 1600 x 1440 per eye, which combined is 2880 x 1600

>> A very generous field of view of 120 degrees

>> A refresh rate that typically hits up to 144 Hz

Most importantly, and what gives the Valve Index much of its higher price tag, is adjustability:

>> The headset includes an *interpupillary distance* (IPD) slider, which lets you change up that value for how wide apart the lenses are as well as an *eye relief* slider (which lets you slide the lenses forward or backward for a perfect fit).

>> You can adjust the headset, so it can fit just about any head.

>> Its built-in audio is immersive and all-encompassing.

You're absolutely getting what you're paying for with the Valve Index. If you pair it with an already-beefy gaming PC, you're going to get some of the best virtual reality gameplay you can currently get on the market.

# Tweaking Game Performance Settings

Flight Simulator includes a dedicated VR performance menu. You can navigate to and tweak the VR settings in this menu to achieve the best flight experience possible in VR mode. After you change up the visual and control settings to your liking, you can set up your VR headset and play the game.

TIP

To proceed with a flight after you achieve the proper VR setup in Flight Simulator, follow the same steps as you would without VR. There are no major menu changes, so you don't need to refamiliarize yourself with the interface.

To access the VR Mode menu, follow these steps:

1. **Choose the Settings tab at the top of your screen.**

2. **In the menu that appears, click the select General Options.**

3. **Choose the VR Mode option from the left column.**

   A VR Mode screen, similar to the one shown in Figure 4-6, appears.

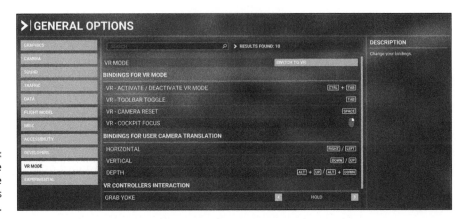

FIGURE 4-6:
A look at the
VR Mode
settings
screen.

In the VR settings screen, you find a wide variety of options that you can adjust to help make Flight Simulator play the best it possibly can in VR. These options enable you to get your Flight Simulator VR experience started off on the right foot by maximizing the game's appearance and performance in VR. Table 4-3 provides a look at some of the options and the settings that support VR play.

**TABLE 4-3** ## VR Settings in Flight Simulator

| Setting | Suggested Value | What the Setting Does |
|---|---|---|
| **Render Scaling** | 90 to 100 | Impacts frame rate and resolution performance. A higher setting gives you the best resolution possible for high-fidelity graphics. Adjust the value downward if you prefer better frame rates, which makes for smoother game play. |
| **Volumetric Clouds** | Medium or High | You're flying around in the sky, so you want the clouds to look their best. Choose Medium to High for the most realistic clouds. |
| **Ambient Occlusion** | Low | This lighting engine setting can cause issues if you set it too high for PCs that can't handle the tech, so keep it low because it does heavily impact some VR rendering performance. |
| **Buildings** | Low to Medium | Controls the number of buildings that the simulator generates. Be conservative with this setting unless you have a high-powered setup. |
| **Reflections** | Low to Medium | Manages the graphic engine's time spent on rendering reflections, such as the shine on glass or water. Keep the setting lower to get better performance. |
| **Terrain Shadows** | 512 | Tweaks the resolution of the shadows that the in-game terrain creates. It greatly affects game performance, especially if you spend time in areas that have more mountains, trees, or plant life. |

| Setting | Suggested Value | What the Setting Does |
|---|---|---|
| **Anti-Aliasing** | TAA | Helps to keep object and texture edges smooth, instead of jagged like you might see in an earlier video game. |
| **Light Shafts** | Low | Controls the number of light shafts that you see, most of which are caused in real life by varying conditions in the atmosphere. |
| **Bloom** | Off | Reduces the effects of luminosity from other light sources in-game. An Off setting helps improve overall game performance because it saves computational power. |
| **Terrain Level of Detail** | 100 | Controls the level of detail of objects on the ground; keep the setting high if you plan on flying low to the ground and want to see everything clearly. |
| **Contact Shadows** | Low | Adjusts and adds shadows to buildings, aircrafts, and some of the other items you see dotting the world. |

IN THIS CHAPTER

» Finding and adding friends to your Flight Simulator escapades

» Creating flight itineraries for multiplayer sessions

» Choosing flights and flight modes

» Actually getting off the ground

» Troubleshooting connectivity issues

Chapter **5**

# Takeoff in Tandem: Flights with Friends

What's better than taking to the friendly skies solo? Flying with friends, of course! In Microsoft Flight Simulator 2020, you can cruise through the sky with friends. Unless you sign up for stunt-flying shows, you probably don't find yourself flying a plane in tandem with someone in real life. You and a trusted friend probably wouldn't even cross paths when zipping along through the air in the real world.

Nothing is much more serene or centering than enjoying the sights from thousands of feet up in the air with someone you love to hang out with. Luckily, inviting someone to explore with you while you soar over the greatest sights across the globe in Flight Simulator isn't a complex or intimidating process.

Flight Simulator approaches multiplayer sessions in a unique way. Originally, the game skipped traditional competitive and cooperative rulesets. Instead, players simply shared the friendly virtual skies while they explored the globe. In the current version of Flight Simulator, you have a variety of options for sharing the experience. For example, you can choose a competitive multiplayer mode, in which you race against your friends.

So, how do you go about bringing a friend into the air with you? This chapter explains that you need only about 10 to 15 minutes to get started with multiplayer flights.

# Meeting up with Friends for a Midair Adventure

What's the first thing you need for a great multiplayer session in Microsoft Flight Simulator? Friends, of course. You can't really enjoy the game with friends when you don't have anyone added to your list of potential wingmen. Before you go planning tandem flights, you need to add the other players whom you want to connect with to your in-game friends list.

## Creating a multiplayer group

Adding friends in Flight Simulator relies on the Microsoft Xbox architecture. You can get the game on both a PC and console; Microsoft publishes it on both platforms. The integrated Xbox app manages your friends list.

**REMEMBER**

If you already have friends whom you added through your profile on Xbox Live, you can simply search for them to add them to your current game.

To add friends to your multiplayer session, follow these steps:

1. **Go to the Flight Simulator main menu by starting the game.**

   If you're already in-game, press the Esc key on your keyboard or the menu button on the controller to make the menu overlay pop up. Select Y or the corresponding button (labeled Main Menu) at the bottom of the screen to return to the main menu.

2. **From the row of icons to the left of your gamertag on the top right of the Main Menu, choose the third one from the left that looks like a single person's head and shoulders.**

   A drop-down list appears that shows all of your Xbox Live friends who currently play Flight on PC or Xbox. The list includes indicators that show whether each friend is currently online or disconnected, as shown in Figure 5-1. If you see the friend whom you want to fly with in the list, skip to Step 5. If you don't see the friend whom you plan on playing with, go on to Step 3 to add them to your friends list.

3. **Select Add Friend from the drop-down list and enter your friend's *Xbox Live Gamertag*.**

Flight Simulator searches its users, and your friend appears via that search function.

**FIGURE 5-1:**
Adding a friend to MSFS 2020.

4. **After you find your friend, send a friend request by highlighting the option and confirming it with a left click or the A button on a controller.**

Receiving a response may take some time unless you're actively in touch with your friend and they accept right away. When your friend accepts your request, their name shows up in your list of online friends (refer to Figure 5-1).

5. **Select your friend's name, and then confirm your selection by left-clicking on it or pressing A on your controller.**

6. **Select the Invite to Group option in the resulting Friend Options drop-down (it's shown in Figure 5-2).**

You and your friend (or friend group, if you chose to add multiple people) can now communicate in-game via the same multiplayer server.

**FIGURE 5-2:**
Viewing your friends or friend group.

**TIP**

You can most easily figure out whether you successfully add a friend to a group for a multiplayer game by looking at the upper-right corner of your game menu. Everyone's icons and profile images appear together at the top of the screen.

## Picking a departure point

After you create a multiplayer group (which you can read about in the preceding section), select the World Map option from the menu on the same screen so that you can prepare a flight.

After you have everyone in your group online and ready to go, and you go to the World Map, look for the icon of the person you're playing with. It appears on the World Map, along with their name in blue lettering in a white box. If a friend is already in-flight, highlight their name, and then select the confirmation button. If you set their name as the Departure option, you can join them mid-flight.

You and your friend (or friends) need to establish a departure point. Here are some things to think about when you do:

>> If no one is flying yet, have all the players in your game agree on a specific departure airport, instead of setting a friend's location on the World Map as your departure point. That way everyone spawns (that is, loads into the game) in their own parking spot instead of awkwardly loading in right behind or beside your friend.

>> When you designate a specific airport for departure, everyone can spawn there without appearing in random areas across the map.

TIP

To help with your departure plans, set up a good communication platform for your multiplayer group. You can communicate with your friends online via the Microsoft Xbox voice chat, but the best way to communicate is through a free third-party app such as Discord. This program enables you to create a free profile and add friends on any platform. You can communicate from your computer or your phone (whether or not you're all currently in-game), and you can also communicate across other video games because chatting on Discord is platform- and app-agnostic.

# Crafting Your Itinerary

After you get your tandem-flying group together (see the section "Meeting up with Friends for a Midair Adventure," earlier in this chapter), you need to choose flight conditions, select an aircraft, and make other important customizations.

Sure, you could just jump into the game and fly somewhere all willy-nilly, but that doesn't give you any semblance of a peaceful flight session. It can also drastically reduce the fun of your flight — unless your entire aim is to be chaotic. (No one's judging you here.) The following sections aim for a smooth multiplayer session, including the options you can choose from when setting up a multiplayer flight.

## Setting flight conditions

After meeting up with friends for your flight, you need to have the game positioned at the World Map. To do so, go to the Main Menu (remember it's the very first screen you see once the game is loaded); then you can move forward from there. Just select the Flight Conditions option at the top right of the screen under your gamertag to get started planning your trip.

From the Flight Conditions screen, as shown in Figure 5-3, you can start choosing the conditions for your flight. Just follow these steps:

1.  **Select one of three options in the Multiplayer section.**

    Your selection sets the overall tone for your entire virtual trip. You can choose

    - *Live Players***:** See only the players who have the same air traffic settings you chose. Simply speaking, this option gives you the most realistic way to play, so if you want to use real-world flight rules, go with Live Players.

    - *All Players:* See all players, no matter what settings they're using. This casual play environment allows everyone to choose their own settings. Although you might find the name of this mode a bit confusing, it means that everyone in your group can choose their own weather, time of day, and other important settings.

    - *Group Only:* Exclude any players not currently in your group. Whoever originally created the group gets to set options such as whether to use Live Weather or custom weather conditions. Those who join the group have to follow the rules of the group creator.

**FIGURE 5-3:** Choosing flight conditions.

2.  **From the Air Traffic section (refer to Figure 5-3), choose an option for the type of traffic you want to experience during your flight.**

Your choices are

- *Live Traffic:* Pulls in data from real-world air traffic. This option offers an experience similar to traffic situations that are going on in the world at that moment. It gives a more simulation-centric, immersive experience.

- *AI Traffic:* Enables the game to generate the type of company you have in the air.

- *Off:* Completely turns off AI air traffic. You experience neither real-world nor generated traffic.

3. **Choose your settings related to Weather and Time from that section in Flight Options.**

   If you don't select the Live Players option in Step 1, then you can tweak these settings. Your options are

   - *Live:* The weather and time of day reflect what's currently going on in your chosen time zone.

   - *Preset:* Choose the weather from a selection of presets.

   - *Custom:* You can change the weather and time of day to your liking. For example, you can change the weather to clear skies, choose Monday at 9:00 a.m., and more. A summary of these customizations appears on the right side of your screen while you choose them.

You can carefully select the flight options that you want to use for your group — or that the group can agree on — based on your preferred operating mechanics.

## Specifying your aircraft and attributes

You still have more to decide after setting up flight conditions (see the preceding section). An important part of flying with friends, just like playing solo, is choosing and configuring the airplane you want to fly. You have a wide variety of airliners, turboprops, jets, and propeller planes to choose from — ranging from the Airbus A320neo to the Cessna Citation CJ4. I believe that picking your aircraft is the most exciting part of this entire setup operation. Chapter 12 outlines the types of planes you can choose from. Honestly, who doesn't want to browse through a cornucopia of planes?

**TIP**

If you want, you can purchase additional planes before jumping into a multiplayer session by way of downloadable content (DLC). The 2020 game release (in the Standard version) originally launched with 20 different aircrafts for all players, although Microsoft and third-party sellers have added numerous aircraft since then. While some of these are free, you have options for purchasing additional aircraft (by visiting the Marketplace on the Main Menu) to add to your menagerie.

Maybe you choose your craft because of aircraft aesthetics or how you feel about the mechanics of a certain airplane.

Keep in mind that the friends joining your session have varying numbers and types of planes that they can choose from. The important consideration is for everyone to fly the craft that they're the most comfortable with, whether that means a massive jet or a smaller propeller plane. You're all playing the game to have fun, after all, and you all can find plenty of fun to be had, no matter what aircraft you're piloting.

Follow these steps to choose and configure your plane:

1. **Locate the Aircraft Selection menu in the top left part of the world map.**

   A menu with a list of blue boxes appears on the left along with images of aircraft options to the right of those boxes, as shown in Figure 5-4.

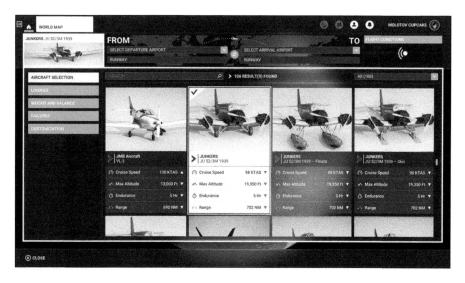

**FIGURE 5-4:** The Aircraft Selection menu.

2. **On the Aircraft Selection main screen, select the plane that you want to fly in this multiplayer session.**

   A small image of each craft appears so that you can see what it looks like at a glance before making your decision.

3. **Specify options that affect the appearance and flight characteristics of your chosen aircraft through the categories in the lefthand column.**

   Your options include

   • *Liveries:* Basically, you can apply a *skin* (outward appearance) to your craft that outfits it with a special design or brand. This option applies to only those aircraft you're flying, but it offers the chance to do some fun customization ahead of your flight.

- *Weight and Balance:* Make adjustments to alter the amount of fuel and weight of the luggage and other cargo aboard your plane. This affects your craft in several ways (see Chapter 13 for more) and may change how you fly it. Figure 5-5 shows all the weights you can enter.

- *Failures:* You can opt in if you want to deal with system failures during the flight, or you can turn them off entirely. Also, establish what kind of failures you want to see: complete system failures, oil system issues, oil leak problems, and/or fuel pump problems. Change the intervals for encountering these system failures or keep them random so that you have to remain on your toes. Chapter 16 offers more about aircraft failures.

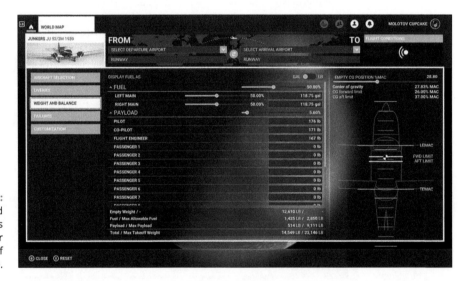

**FIGURE 5-5:**
Weight and balance entries for your airplane of choice.

4. **Decide on and enter your Air Traffic Control (ATC) designation options in the Customization tab.**

   Your ATC options include

   - *Tail number:* Used to identify a particular airplane. For example, N106US.

   - *Flight number:* Usually starts with an abbreviation of the airliner or company flying the plane and a sequence of digits — for example, UA1549 — assigned by the International Air Transport Association (IATA).

   - *Call Sign:* What the air traffic controllers use to address you. Many flight sim enthusiasts use an authentic airline call sign like DELTA or UNITED.

# Siting the all-important destination

For a multiplayer (or solo) flight, you first establish flight conditions and departure point (discussed in the section "Setting flight conditions," earlier in this chapter), and select and configure an aircraft (check out the preceding section). It's time to choose your flight destination. You need to choose the coordinates of the destination that you all have in mind. Because everyone flies to this same location, talk it over with the other players whom you've invited to your game until you reach a unanimous decision.

Picking a common destination may seem difficult at first. You all likely feel paralyzed by the overwhelming number of possibilities. In Flight Simulator, the whole world is your oyster! Figuratively, you can go anywhere you want — so choosing a destination might end up being the most difficult decision you have to make up to this point.

Here are a few fun suggestions that you can try when deciding on where you want to fly with friends:

>> **Someone's home:** Consider flying to your home or a friend's home. Of course, you might want to have a nearby place to land, so flying to an apartment address may not be the best choice. If you opt for a home, make sure there's plenty of open space for landings and takeoffs (if you choose to make a stop).

>> **A landmark:** Look for a landmark that's familiar to all the friends flying with you. For example, a particular skyscraper.

>> **Nearby airports:** Finding a close airport that you all want to explore is a good choice, especially if you want to practice takeoffs and landings.

>> **Major cities:** Perhaps you've always wanted to visit New York, Los Angeles, Tokyo, or London. Why not do so virtually by selecting one of the city's airports as your destination?'

>> **An intriguing sight:** Locations can offer fabulous natural sights, such as Niagara Falls, or manmade sights, such as the Great Wall of China. What sight have you always wanted to see?

>> **A short-distance location:** If you have a limited amount of time for your tandem flight, consider flying to a location that doesn't take long to reach. For example, try flying between the two closest airports.

Your flight destination possibilities are nearly endless. Come to an agreement with your friends about where you're flying — or what you plan on exploring after you lift off and are moving along the flight path. Then select your destination from the World Map, as shown in Figure 5-6.

**FIGURE 5-6:**
Look to the
World Map
for a flight
destination.

# Strategizing and Taking Off

After you gather players and choose important options (such as flight conditions, aircraft, and destination) ahead of liftoff (flip back to the section "Crafting Your Itinerary," earlier in this chapter for the how-to on those options), set a strategy for how you want to reach your destination because not every plane has the same speed or range. Then, guess what? Takeoff time is near!

## Selecting manual control or autopilot

When kicking off a multiplayer session in Flight Simulator, you have a choice about how you want to manage the flying experience. Do you want all the players to manually fly to the destination you select, or do you want to rely on autopilot so that everyone can just enjoy the sights?

Poll your friends to find out whether everyone is comfortable with manual flight. Or maybe they're mostly interested in the experience of getting from point A to point B and seeing the sights while letting the autopilot do the work for them.

REMEMBER

Using autopilot is like taking a virtual airplane ride during which players can look out the windows and even use the game's various camera views to take pictures for posterity.

Decide whether you want to be responsible for the airplane you're flying (manual flight) or just let the game take over (autopilot).

## Starting the tandem flight — finally!

To begin your tandem flight, you just take off like you would for a solo flight. Flying with friends (see Figure 5-7 for a plane that's ready to go) requires no special process or flight screens. You can check out Chapter 8 for a look at accomplishing a successful takeoff.

**FIGURE 5-7:**
Ready for takeoff with your friends.

TEXTRON AVIATION CESSNA 172 SKYHAWK (G1000) - FLOATS

| CRUISE SPEED | 124 KTAS |
| MAX ALTITUDE | 14000 Ft |
| ENDURANCE | 05:00 |
| RANGE | 640 NM |

✈ READY TO FLY

# Collaborating Cross-Console

You can play Flight Simulator on either a PC or Xbox, and the connectivity between these platforms means that any player, regardless of their platform, can jump in and enjoy soaring through the skies in a multiplayer session. Unfortunately, this flexibility also opens up something of a Pandora's box of problems you might experience when fellow players use the other platform.

Long story short, you may encounter some problems when taking a cross-platform tandem flight. My hope is that you come away with a fruitful and exciting online play session with friends. No one should have their flights with friends go down in flames. Er, not flames. You know what I mean. A little pilot humor for you there.

**REMEMBER**

Because of cross-platform conflicts, multiplayer sessions may not always go as smoothly as you want. The same is true for plenty of other multiplayer games. But dealing with platform conflicts in this realistic flight simulator can be a little more frustrating. The problems you encounter during a virtual flight might feel more threatening than, say, disconnecting from a first-person shooter game's deathmatch or being unable to find random players to fill a lobby in a battle royale game.

## Tackling visual and lag issues in multiplayer mode

Sometimes, when you have multiplayer sessions with friends, they don't go entirely swimmingly. That's no big deal; interruptions and lag times can happen with any multiplayer game. If you hop online to play with friends often enough, you probably become intimately familiar with errors and connection problems. But with Flight Simulator, you don't have to sit back and feel miserable because of it.

Table 5-1 includes some simple issues that arise for those trying to take a virtual flight together, as well as a few fixes that can get you up and running in no time.

**TABLE 5-1**     **Common Multiplayer Mode Issues**

| The Problem | What You Do or Don't See | What You Can Do About It |
| --- | --- | --- |
| **Not seeing other players while in multiplayer mode** | You may not see other players often if you aren't exceptionally close to the other planes. But you can have a good idea of where your friends are. | Turn on the Show Traffic Nameplates option. From the main menu, choose Options ⇨ General. Then, under Traffic, choose the Show Traffic Nameplates option to see onscreen notifications that display your friends' names and other flight information. |
| **Not seeing anyone to group up with** | You search for your friends in-game and can't find them. If you know your friends have Flight Simulator, you all may be playing on different instances. | If this is the case, make sure you form a group with your friends beforehand, which guarantees that you all spawn in the same instance. |
| **Experiencing a lag when multiple friends join a session** | Even with a strong Internet connection and a powerful platform, your group experiences lag. Or you experience lag, and the rest of the players are just fine. | Disconnect from the group and enable the Use Generic Plane Models setting. From the main menu, click the Settings tab, and then click Graphics. Toggle on the Use Generic Plane Models option, which can help lessen the system load. Then rejoin the group. |

REMEMBER

You don't have any intimate tech knowledge of online connectivity and platform specs? No problem! You don't have to write any code or do any intensive fixes — leave those things to the experts. But you can work to diagnose your problem and at least try out an easy solution in the meantime.

# Troubleshooting console connectivity

One particularly frustrating issue can happen when players try to connect to or join others' groups in a multiplayer game. If you routinely get disconnected before you can join your friends, you may have a problem with something known as your NAT type.

TECHNICAL
STUFF

*NAT* stands for Network Address Translation. It's one way to measure how your Xbox performs online when connected to your modem or router. Slowdowns, disconnects, and lags in play can be directly related to the NAT type your console displays. You aren't necessarily stuck with the particular NAT type that your console displays; you can change it. However, I encourage you to get technical support from a console expert if you want to mess around with your NAT type.

REMEMBER

NAT type pertains only to the Xbox platform; so if you play Flight Simulator on a PC, your NAT type isn't your lag-time problem.

# 2

# The Art of Single-Engine Navigation

Find out the fundamentals of aircraft attitude — pitch, yaw, and roll — how to deal with physical forces that affect your plane, and how Microsoft Flight Simulator 2020 offers relevant in-game assistance.

Know how cockpit instruments appear, whether digital or analog, and how to monitor and use them in every flight.

Select a beginner aircraft and then get familiar with that plane — as well as popular airports — picking up some advice for taking off and flying, even in adverse conditions.

Discover the art of departing an airport at takeoff, keeping on course, and returning safely to the runway when you're ready.

# Chapter **6**

# Loving Flight Fundamentals

Before you can jump into the cockpit of your chosen plane, it's imperative that you spend some time getting familiar with the fundamentals of flight. Flying involves much more than hopping into the cabin, going hands-on with the control column, and zooming full-speed down the runway until you somehow ascend. If you want to keep your fictional pilot's license, don't do that.

For example, every plane has its own kind of *attitude.* No, I'm not talking about the same sass you might expect from an angsty teenager. The attitude I introduce in this chapter simply describes a plane's orientation in the air. You also need to understand the difference between *pitch, yaw,* and *roll* — which are aspects of your airplane's orientation to the horizon — as well as the aerodynamic forces of *thrust* and *drag* that affect how planes fly.

You may find the more granular aspects of flying more complicated than you first imagined, and to enjoy the freedom of being airborne, you have to provide some extra effort when it comes to figuring out how to handle the airplane. In this chapter, I help you find out about the details of flight mechanics and how the trim systems and other game assistance can help you control your plane.

So, before you set a destination and reach cruising altitude, make sure you understand the concepts that affect the way your plane moves through the sky. After you have a handle on those things, you have a much more complete picture of the inner workings of real-world aircrafts, as well as those in Microsoft Flight Simulator 2020. And that's knowledge that you can use to surprise folks at parties — or on flights.

# Your Plane Will Cop an Attitude

You may be wondering whether your plane is suddenly about to start speaking and get smart with you, a la K.I.T.T. from the TV series *Knight Rider.* Thankfully (or . . . unfortunately?) a plane's attitude has nothing to do with its mood. The term refers to the craft's orientation in terms of where the horizon is located. This position is measured by three principal axes of rotation:

>> **Pitch:** The lateral axis that runs from wingtip to wingtip. This runs horizontally across the midsection of the plane.

>> **Yaw:** The vertical axis that runs from the top to the bottom of the plane's imaginary center of gravity.

>> **Roll:** The longitudinal axis that runs from the nose of the plane to the tail. Think of this as an imaginary line that runs down the plane's midsection.

Imagine these three axes as invisible lines running through the airplane (see Figure 6-1) — bisecting (dividing into two parts) and intersecting (crossing into each other) at various locations throughout — and coming together at the plane's center of gravity. Because keeping an airplane stable and in control is a lot different than driving a car or even a boat, you need to be aware of all three axes at all times. Throwing off even one affects the other two. So to keep your plane in a good humor, as it were, you want to maintain an appropriate attitude, which is comprised of those three types of rotation and related movements.

## Perfecting picture-perfect pitch

*Pitch* refers to the plane's rotation along the imaginary line from wingtip to wingtip. This line is referred to as the *lateral axis.* It's typically controlled by the craft's elevators, of which most planes have two, as shown in Figure 6-2. On most planes, you find the elevators on the back half of the horizontal stabilizer (or the *tail*) on the end of the plane. The elevators create a downward force to help maintain the plane's center of gravity.

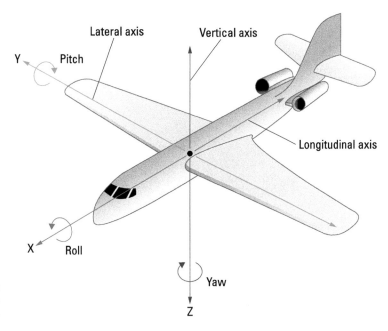

Lateral axis

Vertical axis

Y Pitch

Longitudinal axis

X Roll

Yaw

Z

FIGURE 6-1:
The three axes
of an airplane.

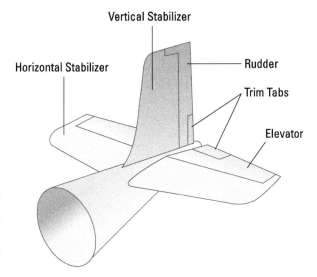

Vertical Stabilizer

Horizontal Stabilizer

Rudder

Trim Tabs

Elevator

FIGURE 6-2:
An aircraft's
parts that help
determine
its position
related to its
axes.

The elevators handle the lateral axis on the outside of the plane. But on the inside, the pilot (that's you!) controls the pitch by using the *yoke* (the control wheel/ control column or stick), as shown in Figure 6-3. Pulling back on the yoke helps pitch the plane nose upward, which creates a *pitch up* attitude for the craft and helps you get the plane into the air. Doing the opposite (pushing downward on the yoke) brings the plane down into a descent. It's easy to remember what pitch does if you think of it like musical pitch: It goes up and down!

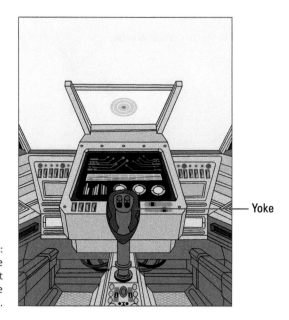

Yoke

FIGURE 6-3:
An airplane
cockpit that
shows the
yoke.

In the Flight Simulator game, how you control the elevators to determine pitch depends upon your setup. If you have a yoke or joystick on a controller, you can use it as you would in a real aircraft. Pushing forward pitches the plane's nose downward and pulling back pitches it upward. If you use the keyboard for your controls, it's a bit harder to control the aircraft because you don't have the advantage of analog movement. Pressing a key will pitch the plane's nose as hard as possible in the direction you choose. So, you must continually tap (and release) a key to make micro adjustments instead of having the smooth motion of a stick. (You can find the specific keyboard controls in Chapter 2).

## Saying yes, yes to yaw

*Yaw* refers to the plane's movement across the *vertical axis* that runs vertically through the top and bottom of the aircraft's center of gravity. Refer to Figure 6-1 for this imaginary line. Put simply, the yaw refers to the plane's twisting motion, left and right.

TIP

If you need an easy way to remember what the yaw does, think of the motion you make when saying no. The universal body language for no has your head yawing from left to right!

Whereas the elevators on your craft control the pitch (see the preceding section), you can rely on the plane's rudders, located on the *fin* (the vertical stabilizer; refer to Figure 6-2) to adjust yaw movement. A *rudder* is basically a miniature wing, similar to what you might see on boats, that works together with ailerons (which find a home on the wings; more about these in the following section) to turn the aircraft along the yaw rotation. Used together, these two mechanisms move in opposite directions to keep the plane flying straight.

You have choices for controlling your virtual rudders and ailerons in Flight Simulator:

TIP

>> **Rudder:** On a keyboard, turn your rudder left with your Num 0 key and right with your Enter key. Console users can use their left and right triggers to control the rudder. In a real-world cockpit, you use foot pedals to move the rudder, but (without accessories) you have to control it with your hands for the purposes of Flight Simulator.

You can also get pedals for Flight Simulator, but incorporating them takes some additional setup time, which may frustrate a beginner who wants to jump in with minimal fuss. Alternatively, you may want to use a controller versus your keyboard. The Xbox controller features analog triggers, which allow for fine controller movements over the rudder versus the simple on-off options the keyboard provides.

>> **Ailerons:** You can typically control your left aileron with the Num 4 key on your keyboard and your right aileron with your Num 6 key. On a controller, you can control the ailerons with your left analog stick. Typically, in the cockpit of a real plane, you use a control wheel or control stick to adjust both ailerons. And similarly to what's available for rudder controller, consider using an Xbox controller for more options when you adjust your ailerons.

## That's how we roll

*Pitch* and *yaw* are two very odd-sounding words for directional movements (see the preceding sections). Here's one that might sound a little less weird: *roll.* The plane's rolling motion rotates around the *longitudinal axis* that goes from the craft's nose all the way to the tail (refer to Figure 6-1). A roll maneuver lets the plane's wings rock from side to side, to the left or right, or even rotate in a complete circle if you're trying some fancy aerobatics — but please don't do this stunt with passengers aboard, even virtual ones.

Roll is controlled by the plane's *ailerons,* or panels that lie near the tip of each wing and can move up and down. They simultaneously create more lift on one wing and reduce lift on the other. They move in the opposite direction of the plane rudder to keep the plane straight (which I talk about a bit more in the preceding section).

## ROLLING WITH FOX McCloud

Here's a fun fact that may help you remember what *roll* refers to when flying a plane. If you've ever played the video game *Star Fox 64*, you likely performed what the game refers to as a *barrel roll* with the Arwing aircraft by pressing one of the Nintendo 64 controller's Z or R buttons twice. However, the maneuver that your pilot, Fox McCloud, performs is actually called an *aileron roll*. Next time someone quotes Fox's teammate saying, "Do a barrel roll!", you can tell them what's *really* up.

To perform an aileron roll to the right, a pilot needs to move up the right aileron, which reduces the lift in the right wing. Doing so makes the left aileron go down, which increases the amount of lift in the left wing. In Flight Simulator, you can achieve a roll to the right by using your Num 6 key or your controller's left analog stick. This maneuver is where the additional fine-tuning an Xbox controller can provide comes in.

### Fine-tuning your plane's performance by using a trim tab

Certain mechanisms on aircrafts can help adjust the plane's interactions with the axes of rotation and aerodynamic forces (see the next section) so that you can maintain the plane's altitude, speed, and direction. The term *trim* refers to doing just that. For example, mechanisms called *trim systems* can help alter the various axes of rotation: pitch, yaw, and roll, described earlier in this section. Out of all of these controls, the pitch trim is by far the most important.

One of the most common trim systems in Flight Simulator is the *trim tab*, or a small, secondary flight control surface that you can find attached to an *elevator, rudder,* or *aileron,* which are external physical parts of the aircraft that control its position. See Figure 6-2 for a look at the trim tab and how it attaches to the other flight control surfaces. You can use the trim tabs to help stabilize the aircraft, and you can adjust these systems in Flight Simulator through the trim knobs commonly found on your yoke or flight stick.

# Exploring Aerodynamic Forces

*Force* is best understood by examining Newton's Third law of Motion, which states that for every action (*force*) in nature, there's an equal and opposite reaction. For example, turning on and engaging an airplane engine creates an action (*thrust*) — movement that pushes the plane forward — to which the response is an opposite reaction (*drag*) that comes from friction and that acts opposite to the direction of motion. When the forces of thrust and drag are balanced, an airplane flies on a level course.

Two other opposite forces, *weight* (caused by gravity) and *lift* (primarily due to wing structure) work with thrust and drag to create the activity we call flight. Together, the two sets of opposing forces are called *aerodynamic forces.*

REMEMBER

When taking to the air in Flight Simulator, you're mostly concerned with thrust and drag because you can directly affect these forces through your game controls.

## Achieving thrust

*Thrust* is an invisible, mechanical force. It's responsible for propelling an airplane forward. Thrust is generated in different ways, depending on whether you're flying a jet engine or a propeller plane. Jet engines use propellers powered by combustion; these propellers create energy that pushes the plane forward. Propeller engines use a turbine blade that spins to create the force that propels your plane forward.

REMEMBER

Regardless of the aircraft, you get thrust from the type of propulsion it uses. And your plane experiences the opposing force — drag (see the following section) — while it's propelled forward.

## Downplaying drag

Bummer: We have to talk about drag now. Just kidding — you don't have to feel down when discussing this type of aerodynamic force. *Drag* opposes an aircraft's motion through the air, and every single bit of the airplane contributes to it. You can think of drag as a type of friction that's produced by air resistance to the airplane's forward motion.

TIP

You can feel drag for yourself when you stick your hand out the window of a car moving at a speed of 25 miles per hour or faster. Hold your palm facing forward, and you can feel your hand pushed back by the air. It also moves up and down if you tilt it. The faster you go, the more you feel this force of drag on your hand.

Unfortunately, drag works to slow your plane's forward momentum (created by thrust) by disrupting any airflow moving around the craft. To decrease drag, a plane must have a streamlined design. You really can't do anything to fight the drag of gravity, but you can lessen the drag caused by wind. A well-designed aircraft directs the wind around the fuselage instead of directly against it, which is the reason why airplanes aren't square blocks.

Because planes are designed to be streamlined, they pass through the air easily and can get up to speed efficiently. But you still need to keep in mind the effects of drag when you're in the cockpit. For example, you retract your landing gear after takeoff to reduce friction (and drag) and make the craft more aerodynamic so that you can gain higher cruising speeds. If you want to remain in the air, you must maintain higher thrust to effectively combat excess drag.

# Don't Be Afraid to Ask for Help

All games have a way for players to get help, but in the case of Flight Simulator, the help goes way beyond telling you how to adjust the volume or fine-tune the controls.

Flight Simulator offers its own type of help with various aspects of flying, so take advantage of it. For example, you can use options on the Assistance menu to streamline landings or make sure your plane doesn't get damaged. With the game's assistance and this book, you're well on your way to becoming a master virtual pilot — or, at the very least, one who gets from point A to point B with relative ease. Hey, everyone's got to start somewhere, right? The content in this section explains what kind of help you can get from the game (and I promise that I'll never tell!).

## Employing in-game assists

You know the controls. You feel confident about the aerodynamics and the forces that act upon your aircraft. You have a copy of this book in your hands — thanks! But don't discount what the game has available to help you. Sometimes, tackling a smooth landing or even communicating with air traffic control (ATC) can feel frustrating or overwhelming. What if I told you that you don't actually have to do any of that if you don't want to? Well, sure, you need to do the landing and communication if you want an authentic simulation experience, but you don't have to handle everything on your own. Look to the Assistance menu for help with these tasks.

REMEMBER

The Assistance menu helps you customize certain parts of the game to make taking flights easier for you. Figure 6-4 shows the Assistance menu, which you can find in your game by clicking the tab (at the upper left) to open the Options menu.

The Assistance menu and its offerings are super useful when you want a more streamlined, simplified flight experience. To get started, follow these steps:

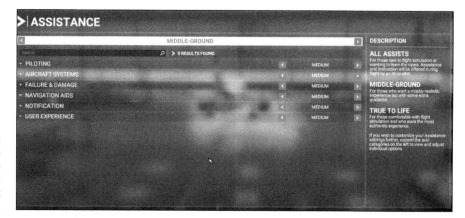

FIGURE 6-4:
A look at the Assistance menu when you first access it.

1. **Go to the Main menu (the first screen in the game).**

   Or toggle the in-game menu on while in-flight by pressing the Escape key or Menu Button.

2. **Select the Options menu from the tabs in the upper left part of the screen.**

3. **From the Options menu, select Assistance.**

   The Assistance menu opens and presents the categories of flight assists that you can customize.

4. **Choose the category that you want to customize.**

   After you choose the category, a variety of options appear that you can use to help make the game easier, more tolerable, or simply tailored to your liking.

   Here are three examples:

   - *Assisted Landing:* If you don't care about getting into the nitty-gritty of the adjustments required for landing and just want to bring that giant bird back to Earth, use the settings in this category. The game actually takes care of all the difficult parts of landing your plane for you: adjusting the throttle, determining flaps percentage, flight trim, airspeed, RPM, and so on. In Assistance window, open the piloting drop-down and turn Assisted Landing on. You can always turn off Assisted Landing later, the same way you turn it on.

   - *Crash Damage:* You can opt to turn off Crash Damage, so if you do happen to run into any buildings or the ground, your plane isn't affected. Open the Failure & Damage drop-down and disable Crash Damage.

   - *Unlimited Fuel:* If you don't want to run out of fuel, toggle on Unlimited Fuel so that it never becomes a concern. Open the Aircraft Systems drop-down and toggle on Unlimited Fuel from there.

# Checking out all the assists

It's all about flying smarter, not harder. Unless you're looking to use Flight Simulator to help you prepare for real flight school; then, you might want to grin and bear the harder parts. You don't have any of these assists up in the real skies.

Table 6-1 gives you a rundown of all the Assistance categories and options that you can pick and choose from.

**TABLE 6-1**    ## Assistance Categories and Options

| Category | Option | How You Use It |
|---|---|---|
| Aircraft Systems | Automixture | Without this option turned on, you adjust the mixture of fuel and air in your plane's engine by using the Mixture lever. (While you go higher, air pressure changes, requiring changes in the ratio of fuel to air.) If you turn on this feature, the game handles this adjustment for you. |
| | Unlimited Fuel | This option is self-explanatory. You don't have to worry about refueling. |
| | Aircraft Lights | Flight Simulator automatically controls your aircraft lights. |
| | Gyro Drift Auto-Calibration | The game completes your gyro drift calibration for you. If you don't complete this calibration, your compass and other navigational instruments might lose precision. |
| Failure & Damage | Crash Damage | Your plane doesn't take damage in a crash if you toggle this option off. |
| | Aircraft Stress Damage | You can turn *stress damage,* or damage incurred by pushing your craft to its limits, on or off. If you overstress your plane and this option is on, you see a black screen that tells you so. |
| | Engine Stress Damage | You can turn *engine stress damage,* or damage done by pushing the engine as far as it can go, on or off. |
| | Icing Effect | Turn on or off visible ice that appears on your aircraft. |
| Navigation Aids | Route and Waypoints | Choose whether you want to see your route or waypoints for each trip visualized in the game world. |
| | Taxi Ribbon | Choose whether you want to see a navigational ribbon showing you where to begin taxiing on the runway of an airport. |
| | Landing Path | Choose whether you want to see the landing path that you need to take laid out onscreen. |
| | Smartcam Mode | Turn this option on to have the camera automatically focus on the closest point of interest. |

| Category | Option | How You Use It |
|---|---|---|
| | POI Markers | Choose whether you want to see point-of-interest (POI) markers on your map when flying around the world. |
| | City Markers | Choose whether you want to see city markers displayed when exploring the globe. |
| | Airport Markers | Choose whether you want to see airport markers displayed across the globe. |
| | Fauna Markers | Choose whether you want to see areas with fauna and flora marked when flying around. |
| Notification | Piloting and Controls Notifications | Toggle piloting and control notifications on or off. When on, these notifications appear as pop-ups. |
| | Aircraft System | Turn aircraft system notifications on or off. |
| | Flying Tips | Turn flying tips during play on or off. |
| | Objectives | Decide whether you want to be notified of different objectives per mission. |
| | Software Tips | Toggle software tips on and off. |
| User Experience | ATC UI Panel Open at Start | Choose whether you want the air traffic control (ATC) panel to open onscreen when you start your flight. |
| | Show Message Log in ATC Menu | Choose whether you want to show your prior message log from ATC in the main menu. |
| | ATC Voices | Turn the ATC voices on or off. |
| | Checklist in UI Panel open at start | Choose whether you want your flight checklist in your UI panel to open when you start your flight. |
| | VFR Map UI Panel open at start | Choose whether you want to see the visual flight rules map open up onscreen when you start your flight. |
| | Nav Log UI Panel Open at Start | Choose whether you want to display your navigation log UI panel when you start your flight. |

# Letting the game work for you

In the same menu area where you can turn on Assistance options (see the preced-ing section), you can also find a submenu called Flight Assistant (see Figure 6-5) that contains AI Controls, which offer various ways to put the game to work doing things that you otherwise have to handle yourself.

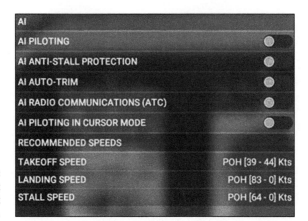

FIGURE 6-5:
The Flight
Assistant
menu.

REMEMBER

With AI Controls, you essentially make the game your copilot. These options don't offer assistance — they're straight-up doing things for you. That way, you really only have to worry about flying to cool destinations, checking out new planes, and enjoying the beautiful sights all around you.

Follow these steps to access the AI Control settings to make the game work for you:

1. **While in-flight, toggle the menu toolbar at the top of the screen.**

   Either press Ctrl + C on your keyboard or press down on the left stick on your Xbox controller.

2. **Choose a setting from the floating menu that appears.**

   You have three options: Checklist Assist, Manage Radio Comms, and Control Aircraft.

3. **Press Enter (on your keyboard) or A (on your Xbox controller) to confirm which option you want to activate.**

   Flight Simulator gets you back in your flight with the option you selected in Step 2 active.

When activated, the game's artificial intelligence (AI) controls each setting. Here's a description of each one:

>> **Checklist Assist:** Activating this setting means that the AI takes care of everything you need to do before and after takeoff: pulling up your landing gear, turning off your parking brake, and every other important safety check you need before being turned loose into the air. You may find all the work involved in getting going tedious, so the game can take it off of your hands.

>> **Manage Radio Comms:** This setting does just what it says: It takes care of any communication that you need to have with the air traffic control tower. Without this setting activated, you need to spend quite a bit of time sending over flight details before and during your trip, especially when landing. With this option activated, however, your AI copilot has your back.

>> **Control Aircraft:** This setting removes any responsibility for the flight from you so that you can kick back, relax, and cruise. Your AI copilot handles the plane and every aspect of the flight, from simple to complex flight plans and everything in between. Activate this option if you want to complete a trip and just be along for the ride, or if you don't really want to play, you just want the vibe.

Make the game do what you want it to — you don't always have to be in charge if you don't want to be.

Chapter **7**

# Learning Those Instruments

To successfully fly in Microsoft Flight Simulator 2020, you need to know how to use the various instruments included in your cockpit. At first, getting to know and understand each instrument may seem confusing. But, with a little time and guidance, you can discover what every instrument does, as well as how to read it during flight.

The instruments in Flight Simulator can tell you how fast you're going (*airspeed*), how high up you are (*altitude*), and other vital information that you need to know, such as the direction you're flying (your *current heading*).

Flight Simulator has two primary types of cockpits that you can become acquainted with:

» **An analog cockpit** relies on *analog instruments* that appear as dials and gauges and rely on mechanical measurements to display information. You need to know how to read the various needles and indicators that relay these measurements.

» **A glass cockpit** relies on multiple electronic panels to sift through and display important information to you digitally during flight. This means you'll get a direct readout rather than you having to interpret analog dials and gauges.

In this chapter, you can explore how to read and use the instruments in an analog cockpit, as well as how to read and interact with your instruments in a glass cockpit.

Grab your go-bag and let's get started.

# Reading Analog Instruments

Many of the planes in Flight Simulator have analog cockpits, especially the older planes. In fact, many of the planes that you fly during the game's tutorial lessons rely on analog instruments for vital information such as heading, altitude, and so on. For that reason alone, you need to know how to read analog instruments early on in your career with Flight Simulator.

However, some planes are hybrids with a combination of analog and digital systems. For example, the Cessna 172 includes a digital radio and navigation system but uses analog gauges for nearly everything else.

TIP

Coming to terms with the instruments in your aircraft is about identifying each panel — where it is and what it does. Although a cockpit may look daunting at first, knowing the basics of each instrument (position and function) can make your flights easier in the long run.

Overall, the exact layout, functionality, and appearance of instruments may vary depending on your aircraft. However, several fundamental instrument types are in each cockpit, so get acquainted with them. For this example, I present the cockpit of a Cessna 152, as shown in Figure 7-1.

The callouts in Figure 7-1 correspond with some of the instruments in this list:

>> **Airspeed indicator:** Displays your *airspeed* (how fast you're traveling), measured in *knots* (which is one nautical mile per hour). Pay special attention to this instrument during flight because aircraft are very sensitive to speed. For example, unlike cars, which will just stop in one place if you run out of speed, an airplane will drop like a rock. This situation is obviously bad for the pilot. The white lines on the airspeed indicator signal that you can extend the flaps at those speeds.

Remember that the higher the speed, the lower the *tilt* (using the rudders to pivot the plane up or down). The green line marks the speed range in which you can safely tilt the rudders at their full range of movement. The yellow range means you're quickly approaching the limit of the plane's structural strength.

Attitude indicator          Altimeter

Airspeed indicator          Vertical Speed indicator

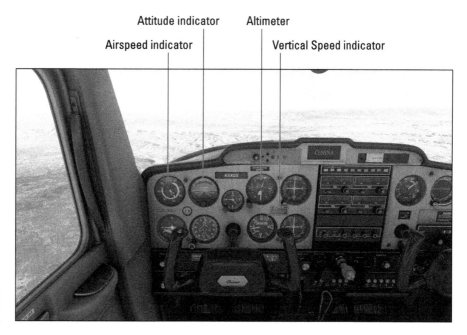

FIGURE 7-1
A view of an
analog cockpit.

>> **Attitude indicator:** Shows the current orientation of the plane in space. You make use of this instrument when you have to fly based on your instruments to ensure your angle of approach does not exceed recommendations. The brown portion in this indicator signifies the ground, and the blue part indicates the sky.

>> **Altimeter:** Shows you the current *ceiling* (meaning the maximum density altitude an aircraft can reach) in feet or meters. Keep in mind that the altimeter measures the elevation of your craft Above Sea Level (ASL). Just because you're on the ground doesn't mean that you have an altimeter value of zero. When your craft is on the ground, the altimeter shows a value of anywhere from a few hundred feet to several thousand feet, depending on the elevation above sea level of the airport you're currently visiting.

TIP

Before takeoff, tune the altimeter to the barometric pressure at the airport's location. Chapter 3 explains how to make this adjustment and indicates its importance as a pre-takeoff step.

>> **Throttle RPM meter:** Shows you the current revolutions per minute (RPMs) of the plane's engine.

>> **Flaps control:** Controls the flaps on the rear of the wings. Essentially, you can adjust these mechanisms to provide more load-bearing force — allowing the plane to take off from a shorter distance — or keep the plane airborne at a low speed. Chapter 6 goes into the flaps and other physical parts of an airplane. Additionally, flaps may be used to slow down the plane.

- » **Fuel Mixture control:** Regulates how much fuel is injected into the engine. You need to reduce or increase the ratio of fuel to air being injected, depending on the altitude and density of the air that you're flying through.

- » **Throttle:** The throttle is pretty self-explanatory; it's essentially your gas pedal. It controls the amount of fuel and air that is being injected into the engine. The more open the throttle, the more power the engine produces. Unlike cars, which have a gearbox to transfer power to the wheels, airplanes are direct drive, which means an increase in throttle always manifests as a higher RPM.

- » **Pitch Trim:** By far one of the most important mechanisms in the cockpit. When set correctly, it allows the plane to fly without the pilot having to continuously hold the steering bar (also called the *yoke*). You may need to make adjustments to the pitch trim (which maneuvers the aircraft elevators) constantly throughout the flight in order to maintain altitude or a steady climb or decent.

- » **Vertical Speed indicator:** Showcases the current speed of ascent or descent. It measures your plane's speed in feet per minute. This instrument never sticks rigidly in one place; expect it to fluctuate. When landing or ascending, the standard rate of speed on this instrument varies from plane to plane.

- » **Current Heading:** Shows the aircraft's current heading course throughout the flight. The *heading* is essentially the direction that the aircraft is traveling relative to the magnetic north. The cardinal headings include

  - *North* at 360 or 0 degrees

  - *East* at 90 degrees

  - *South* at 180 degrees

  - *West* at 270 degrees

  The Current Heading indicator itself gets input from a gyroscope, so you can expect it to show the wrong direction when not calibrated properly. Unfortunately, it becomes misaligned by itself often, and you need to calibrate it throughout your flight by resetting it every 10 to 15 minutes and ensuring it lines up with your compass.

- » **Parking Brake:** The parking brake is exactly what it sounds like. Use it at every takeoff and taxi situation to avoid any issues with air traffic control (ATC; see Chapter 10). Remember, when your aircraft's engine is on, it generates thrust, even at idle. If you don't make sure your parking brake is on, you may look down to hit a switch and find you're rolling along.

# Going Digital in a Glass Cockpit

Despite being based on digital screens (which many people know from their computers, smartphones, and tablets), a glass cockpit may actually come across as more confusing than analog instruments when you first start using them. Glass cockpits rely on a few displays to showcase a lot of different bits of information. Because of the multiple displays, you need to shift through different screens to get a look at all the information you need throughout your flight.

In glass cockpits, you often have a primary flight display (PFD) and a multifunction flight display (MFD). Each one showcases different features and instruments, so keep that in mind when you select an aircraft that has this type of instrument setup.

The glass cockpits in Flight Simulator are mostly based off of Garmin devices, which have two screens that are around 10.4 inches wide. Like analog cockpits, the layout of these displays can vary depending on the aircraft model. However, they involve similar elements.

TIP

Take your time memorizing the layout of your aircraft cockpit's instruments. I recommend completing multiple flights by using the same aircraft, which allows you to solidify your memory about where each instrument is and how to access the information that you need for a successful flight.

## The primary flight display (PFD)

The primary flight display (PFD) is the main screen that you must pay attention to during flight. (Figure 7-2 shows an example PFD from a Boeing 747.) It's located on the left of the cockpit (where the pilot in command sits) and can be replicated on the right for the copilot. By default, the PFD displays all the basic information that's related to your flight, such as altitude, heading, speed, and so on.

Usually, the PFD shows you a GPS map, an airspeed indicator, an indicator for your autopilot modes, and several other features. Here's a brief overview of what to expect on this screen:

>> **GPS map:** Gives you an idea of the terrain around you, including hills, mountains, and so on. You can change the scale of the map by using the controls at the bottom of the display. This map also shows the true airspeed (TAS) and ground speed (GS).

>> **Airspeed indicator:** Shows you the aircraft's current speed in knots.

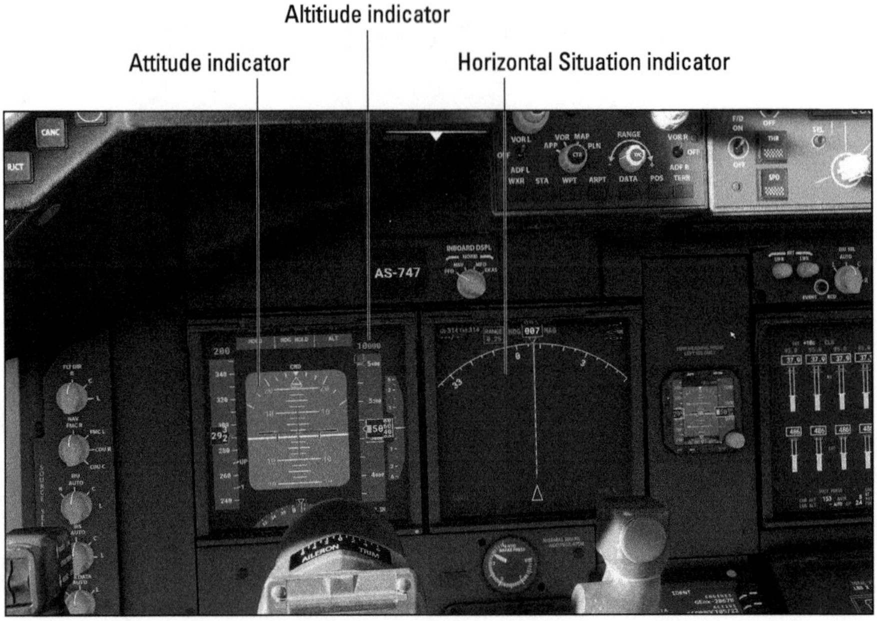

Altitiude indicator

Attitude indicator

Horizontal Situation indicator

**FIGURE 7-2:**
A view of
a glass
cockpit's PFD.

>> **Angle of Attack:** Don't let the name fool you; this display has nothing to do with combat. However, the *angle of attack* — the angle of the wings' inclination relative to the air that's flowing around them — is an important bit of data to take into account during flight. For example, if your angle of attack is too high, you'll lose airspeed and quickly stall the aircraft.

>> **Autopilot Mode indicators:** Show you what mode of autopilot (if any) the aircraft is currently set to.

>> **Attitude indicator:** Check this to see the aircraft's current position as it relates to the horizon.

>> **Horizontal Situation indicator:** An extended version of the *compass rose* (a circle illustrating the principal directions printed on a map or chart). Not only does it show compass directions (north, south, east, and west), but it also displays the current heading for the aircraft (for example, 030) in large white lettering. It also shows the heading bug (or HDG) set for autopilot and the Course (CRS) to the nearest GPS navigation point from your flight plan.

>> **Altitude indicator:** Displays the aircraft's current altitude above sea level (ASL). *Note:* For accuracy, don't forget to change the current barometric pressure based on what ATC tells you before takeoff.

>> **Distance and Course indicator:** Displays the course and distance to the currently selected GPS navigation point.

The overall look and layout of the PFD can change, depending on which aircraft you're flying. Sometimes, the display is surrounded by buttons on either side. Often, you use these buttons only to operate the Autopilot functionality and adjust the radio. You can usually adjust other parameters, such as the scale of the GPS map and more, by using these buttons, too.

## The multifunction flight display (MFD)

The second screen in your aircraft that you need to pay attention to, after the primary flight display (see the preceding section), is the multifunction flight display (MFD). This display can mimic many of the same points as the PFD.

By default, you can expect to see this kind of layout for your aircraft's MFD:

>> **GPS map:** The same map showcased on the PFD. You can replace the GPS map with a weather radar display if you prefer. How you make this replacement depends on the aircraft itself.

>> **Engine Operation indicators:** Showcases the current engine RPM, oil pressure, engine temperature, and other important engine information.

>> **Current Navigational Data:** Displays information about the current navigation point that you selected from your flight plan. This panel includes information such as distance from the navigation point, estimated time of arrival (ETA), and so on.

>> **Trim and Flap indicators:** This small section showcases the current settings of the pitch, trim, and flaps of the aircraft. You need this information to fine-tune your aircraft's flight.

REMEMBER

If you want to change the information that appears on the MFD, you can use the buttons or touch panel below the display. The options vary, depending on which model of aircraft you're flying.

TIP

If you find yourself struggling with glass cockpits, or if they seem daunting, keep in mind that many of them contain analog indicators for the primary flight information, including altitude, speed, and so on. Using these analog helpers can get you comfortable with using the larger digital display screens, especially in new aircraft.

Chapter **8**

# Pulling Off a Successful Start-Up

No matter how many virtual flights you take in Microsoft Flight Simulator 2020, you encounter two flight stages — takeoff and landing — that can be challenging for their own reasons. Both of these parts of any flight rely on your (the pilot's) skill, especially when you start dealing with larger or more complex aircraft.

But how do you know what type of aircraft to choose first? And, how do you know when you're prepared to take off? This chapter details the basic necessities to keep in mind when preparing for takeoff, including how to get your bearings around the airport that you're departing from. (Check out Chapter 9 for the lowdown on making a landing.)

# Choosing a Good Starter Plane

One of the first things you need to do when preparing to head out on a flight is choose the aircraft that you want to fly. Figure 8-1 shows the screen where you select an aircraft. Although Flight Simulator gives you several aircraft to choose from, I recommend starting with the Textron Aviation Cessna 152 because it has a simple cockpit layout and is forgiving in the air.

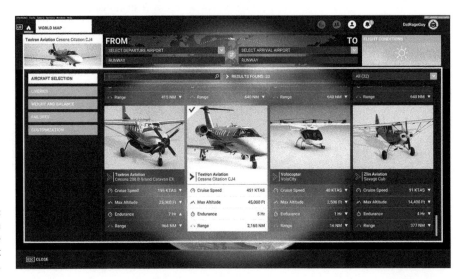

FIGURE 8-1:
Choose a
proper plane
for your first
flight.

The Cessna 152 has a max altitude of 14,700 feet and an endurance of five hours. It can travel a maximum range of only 415 nautical miles, but that's more than enough distance for you to cover on your first few flights.

**TIP**

One of the main reasons for choosing this plane is its ease of operation for the required tasks of takeoffs and landings, and also while just flying from point to point. After you're comfortable with flights in the Cessna 152, you can try out the much larger and more complex planes — such as a Citation CJ4 jet or an Airbus A320neo airliner — that Flight Simulator offers players. Chapter 12 gives you a rundown of the types of planes that you can choose from and their unique characteristics.

Because the Cessna 152 is simpler than many other aircraft, it's a good choice to help you get used to the cockpit controls and the feel of the aircraft on the runway. And it glides well through the air, too.

# Looking around Your Departure Airport

After you choose your plane, it's time to take note of your surroundings. Before you start requesting clearance to taxi or anything like that, look around the airport that you selected as your departure point. (Make this selection by choosing the airport from the World Map menu or entering the airport identifier in the search box.) Figure 8-2 shows an airport and a plane near the gate.

Keep an eye out for important airport signage — such as lanes and taxiway designations — because signage is the best way to tell at any given moment exactly where in the airport you are. Look for taxiway lines, which are yellow and resemble the lines you might see on a standard roadway. You can follow these lines while you taxi out to certain runways and places in the airport. Also, pay attention to things such as gates and other important landmarks at the airport — including the air traffic control (ATC) tower.

When navigating the airport, look for the different types of signs. Signs that have yellow backgrounds and black text, as shown in Figure 8-3, represent taxiways that you're about to cross. These signs tell you which way to turn to access each taxiway, so you can easily move to the taxiway that ATC tells you to use. (See Chapter 10 for information on the standard features you find at an airport.)

Signs that have a black background and yellow text (see Figure 8-4) indicate the taxiway that you're currently on. Some of these signs may offer numbers after the taxiway's designation: For example, numbers after a taxiway designation mean that it's going to intersect with a runway. Alternatively, a taxiway sign might have yellow boxes with a group of letters and an arrow. This indicates an intersection is coming up and lets you know where each direction out of the intersection leads.

Finally, signs featuring a red background and white text represent critical parts of the airport. These signs, as shown in Figure 8-5, appear predominantly on runways and important areas that require specific clearance to enter. You also often see yellow lines along the ground to indicate where to stop your aircraft if you haven't yet received ATC clearance to enter the runway.

# Heading to (or from) Popular Airports and Landmarks

If you're looking for iconic destinations — whether it's for the sheer epic size of the airport itself or the vistas around it — Flight Simulator gives you great places to choose from. We've curated a couple especially good spots and go over each in the following sections, so make sure to check them out when planning your flights. You can also flip to Chapter 19 for even more interesting airports to visit.

## Hong Kong International Airport (VHHH)

If you want to take off or land in an airport that shows off the sheer size of the cities that man has built up, you can't find much better than Hong Kong International, shown in Figure 8-6. It's International Air Transport Association (IATA) identifier code is VHHH. Located just west of the city proper, this airport gives you a perfect view of Hong Kong itself, which is one of the most densely populated places on the planet. The city looks very impressive, especially when you're taking off from Hong Kong International at night.

## Maria Reiche Neuman Airport (SPZA)

Ever heard of the Nazca Lines? Located in the Nazca Desert of Peru, these man-made, ancient geoglyphs are absolutely spectacular from the sky. And you can actually reach them very easily by starting or ending your flight at Maria Reiche

Neuman Airport (shown in Figure 8-7; the IATA code is SPZA). The airport itself isn't much to look at compared to some others, but it's located just east of the Nazca Lines, which you can get a gorgeous view of from the sky.

FIGURE 8-6: You don't have to travel far to get a view of Hong Kong from this airport.

FIGURE 8-7: Taking off from the Maria Reiche Neuman Airport offers a view of the Nazca Lines in Peru.

# Preparing for and Accomplishing Takeoff

After you choose your plane (which we talk about in the section "Choosing a Good Starter Plane," earlier in this chapter) and determine your departure location and destination (see the section "Heading to (or from) Popular Airports and Landmarks," earlier in this chapter), you're ready to actually get off the ground. To help get your plane in the air, you can pick up on know-how about taking off and landing in Chapter 9. For the purpose of this section, we assume you already taxied out to the runway and have clearance to take off from the air traffic controller. (Chapter 11 takes you through the ins and out of communicating and taking departure directions from ATC.)

## Checking your flaps, releasing the parking brake

Prior to takeoff, check the position of your flap by interacting directly with the Flap handle in your cockpit. Because you're preparing for takeoff, place the handle in what pilots refer to as the *first notch* by advancing it one position or pressing the increase flaps key (F7) or button (D-Pad Up). This first-notch position of the flaps on the wings, as shown in Figure 8-8, gives your airplane the maximum amount of lift with the least amount of added drag. (Chapter 6 gives you the low-down on aerodynamic forces — such as lift and drag — that affect flying.)

First notch of flaps

**FIGURE 8-8:** Extending the flaps enough for lift but not too much to create excess drag.

After you set your flaps, ensure they're in place by either looking out the window, using the external camera, or checking your digital readout (if equipped), go ahead and release the parking brake by either pressing Ctrl + Num Del on the keyboard or the Y/B button on the Xbox controller.

Not sure where to find the Num Del key on your keyboard? Check out the period (.) key on the number pad — it also displays Del in small letters. To use the Del function of this key, you need to turn your keyboard's Num Lock off by pressing the Num Lock key.

## Centering up on the runway

To ensure that you have a clear view of everything that's happening in- and outside of the aircraft, before you start bumping up the throttle, take a moment to situate your camera nicely in the cockpit. To do so press Ctrl+Space or press in on the right analog stick. Make sure your view looks something like the view in Figure 8-9.

**FIGURE 8-9:** Give yourself a good view of everything before taking off.

Adjust the camera so that you can easily see your important instruments and also have the maximum view possible when looking out the cockpit window. Also, ensure that you situate and center your yoke or stick by just letting go of it. If you lined up with the runway and centered, when you start throttling up, you don't have to worry about immediately riding off the runway.

# Triggering the thrust

With your view centered in the cockpit and your aircraft centered on the runway (we explain setting that up in the preceding section), you can start applying *thrust* (generating energy to propel the aircraft) by adjusting the throttle (moving it forward) to increase power to the engine. This action results in your plane's forward motion.

TECHNICAL STUFF

You are really increasing the fuel-air mixture in the engine when you increase the throttle, which results in more power being generated. This, in turn, increases your engine's RPMs, which makes the propellers spin faster. So with that in mind, thrust is more of a by-product of increasing the throttle instead of a direct result.

REMEMBER

Start increasing the throttle gently at first and observe your progress down the runway to help ensure that you're actually situated correctly on the runway (meaning centered; see Figure 8-10). But you have only one chance to take off without issue — and runways don't go on forever — so try not to take too long to establish position.

FIGURE 8-10: Ensure you're centered on the runway before attempting takeoff.

After you're sure that you're centered on the runway, you can cautiously turn up the heat. Take the throttle and increase it at a steady pace — not too quickly or too slowly.

## Putting the pedal to the metal

When you've increased the throttle enough (the speedometer shows when the plane is traveling at the correct speed for liftoff, known as *Vr)* go ahead and start pulling back on the yoke. Doing so tips the nose of the aircraft into the air, which is how you generate the lift that you need to take off.

**TECHNICAL STUFF**

Additionally, *V1* is known as the *commit-to-fly* speed; the pilot needs to decide at this speed whether to continue flight if an engine has failed. *V2* (also known as the takeoff safety speed) is the speed needed for the airplane to climb if there is an engine failure.

Depending on the departure airport, the runways vary in length. Be aware of whether your runway is long or short; you need to pull up sooner on a shorter runway than you do if you have more runway room.

**REMEMBER**

Ultimately, your goal is to increase your throttle and get the aircraft off the ground. Remember that the larger the aircraft, the more thrust and lift required to get it off the ground. Starting with a smaller aircraft can help you achieve a successful takeoff much more easily.

# Handling Adverse Flying Conditions

A successful flight isn't completely dependent on pilot skill and a plane's mechanical reliability. Sometimes pilots have to contend with issues, such as low visibility, which can occur outside of human control. Flight Simulator tests your piloting skills the most during these unexpected moments.

## Blame it on the weatherman

One thing that you might forget to take into account when planning your takeoff is the weather. Adverse weather conditions are a part of every pilot's life, and as a pilot, you're going to need to figure out how to plan for and pay attention to possible threats from the weather. Figure 8-11 shows a storm front that you must navigate safely to reach your destination intact.

FIGURE 8-11:
Bad weather
can pose a
significant
challenge for
pilots looking
to take off.

When taking off in inclement weather — such as thunderstorms and high winds — remember to keep the wind's speed and direction in mind, as well as the effects of precipitation. Figure 8-12 shows an airport windsock that indicates the direction and strength of the wind. Adverse weather conditions can completely change how you take off with your aircraft, especially if you're using a smaller aircraft. For example, suppose that you

>> **Experience a *crosswind*** (one that blows across the runway). In this case, you need to use your rudder to compensate for being pushed sideways.

>> **Have a strong *tailwind*** (one that blows from behind the aircraft). Consider throttling down to avoid overspeeding.

>> **Encounter rain-slick runways.** Look out for slick runways by watching for the glint of light from the water on them; the rain can make these runways difficult to navigate.

Ultimately, the weather is a bit out of your control, unless you change the settings within the game by accessing the weather settings in the top bar. If you figure out how to deal with adverse weather conditions, though, you can take off during *almost* any type of weather.

## Cautious night flying

Flying at night can be dangerous because aircraft, like other vehicles such as cars, aren't exactly easy to see when it's pitch-black outside.

Windsock

FIGURE 8-12:
Wind speed
and direction
are important
factors that
affect takeoff.

Luckily, on-craft lights and blinkers can help other pilots see where your plane is, so make sure to use them. The exact location of the light switches can change depending on the plane you're flying, but make sure you always turn on your exterior lights, your logo lights, and your wingtip indicators. For example, in the Cessna 152 that I recommend in the section "Choosing a Good Starter Plane," earlier in this chapter, you find the light controls near the yoke.

WARNING

If you take off and fly at night, keep an eye out for any landmark obstacles and large landforms — such as mountains. Depending on the plane you're flying, you may not be able to fly over the taller mountain ranges of the world, for example. Instead, you may need to modify your course to fly around them. My recommendation is to know what obstacles might be in your path *before* you take off.

Chapter **9**

# Departing from and Returning to the Runway

Departing from and returning to the runway are both crucial parts of flying in Microsoft Flight Simulator 2020 (and of flying in real life, as well). And, because these flight segments are so vital, they both have multiple aspects that you need to be aware and mindful of when doing either.

For example, you need to learn how to navigate through the airport correctly when heading to the runway to take off. And landing requires that you work with air traffic control (ATC) to avoid surrounding air traffic while you approach the airport.

In this chapter, I break down several important factors to consider when taking off or landing at an airport. These factors include tips about how to slow down your airspeed, what kind of patterns to use when landing, and even how to keep your bearings straight on the runway.

## Making It Up into the Air

Getting off the ground is one of the first major hurdles that you face as a pilot in Flight Simulator. First, take some time to go over the basic controls that you have to work with for takeoff — controls such as flaps, the parking brake, stick (or yoke), throttle, and other necessities introduced in Chapter 8. After you feel familiar and comfortable with these basic controls, it's time to get your plane moving and actually prepare for taking off, as shown in Figure 9-1.

FIGURE 9-1:
Landing and taking off present you with controls to conquer and obstacles to overcome.

## Finding and staying the course

Airports need to be extremely organized; and to remain that organized, the pilots behind the sticks must be able to follow basic patterns and expected routes around the various taxiways and runways. But, as you probably already know, no two airports have facilities and layout that are exactly alike. So, how do you make sure that you're following the correct patterns and bearings?

First, pay attention to any signage around the runways that you're crossing over. Keep an eye out for specific signs, which point you towards the runway that you've been assigned to for takeoff. Figure 9-2 shows how signage can point the way. If you're starting from the takeoff point on the runway, then you don't have to worry about figuring out how to taxi. However, you still need to keep your bearing straight and centered, even after you're on the runway.

REMEMBER

Keeping your aircraft centered in the runway might sound easy, but it's actually quite difficult — especially when you start throttling up and preparing to actually leave the ground. One of the easiest ways to center your aircraft is to move your camera to the center of your cockpit (Chapter 2 covers key controls for the cockpit camera). Some pilot seats may be shifted to the left or right drastically, depending on the cockpit design. This is similar to the interior of an automobile, where a definite driver's side exists.

FIGURE 9-2:
Signage
around
airports tells
you where
to go.

After you center the camera, you can more easily point the nose of the aircraft down the center of the runway. Then, try to keep the nose as centered as possible after you start the takeoff process.

## Attending to alignment correction and vertical stabilization

In this chapter, I don't repeat all the basics of taking off; see Chapter 8 for the details of getting off the ground. But, after your aircraft leaves the runway, you must complete the departure process.

The departure process can change, depending on what flight rules you're using (VFR or IFR, see Chapter 11) and what airport you're leaving. For the most part, after takeoff, simply maintain a stable course heading with a steady climb and speed. Doing so can be difficult due to the need to balance vertical and horizontal speed, and you need to keep even pressure on the stick to keep the aircraft from pitching downward, as shown in Figure 9-3. If your plane does pitch downward (see Chapter 6 for the lowdown on pitch), you can lose a lot of your upward momentum and may even crash the aircraft — and you don't want to let that happen.

REMEMBER

If you are on a plane with autopilot, that function can handle the balance situation for you. Autopilot, ideally, eliminates any need for you to balance speed and pitch.

**FIGURE 9-3:**
Try not to pitch
down when
taking off; it
can slow your
climb.

**TIP**

To avoid a downward pitch while climbing, keep the aircraft throttled at the same speed that you used during takeoff. For some smaller aircraft, this speed is around 55 knots. Other larger planes may require more speed to get them off the ground completely. And be careful not to *pitch up too high* — that is, don't pull back on the stick (or yoke) too much — because that can cause a decrease in airspeed. You want the aircraft to maintain speed while also climbing, so you may need to practice finding that perfect balance point between pitch and throttle for both climbing and maintaining speed.

Another factor to consider is your plane's current *vertical stability* — the positioning that keeps the aircraft flying straight ahead — and whether you need to compensate for it. A vertical stabilizer keeps the nose of the plane from moving side to side, which is a movement called *yaw* (see Chapter 6 for more on yaw). To adjust for vertical stability, you can trim the rudder when needed.

**REMEMBER**

If you aren't climbing as quickly as you should, or if you're causing the aircraft to *redline* (reach an airspeed above which flying is unsafe), you may experience issues that can knock you off course or out of the sky. Make careful and gentle course and speed corrections by using the throttle and elevators. Also, be sure to maintain the same speed and pitch up after taking off until reaching your cruising altitude, at which point you can level off.

## Maintaining speed and climbing

You need to maintain your speed while climbing (as I discuss in the preceding section) for any aircraft, but especially for larger aircraft. You're essentially lifting a massive metal bird that can't flap its wings off the ground. Having a sufficient and stable speed ensures that you don't run into problems keeping your aircraft off the ground.

Some adjustment of pitch and throttle may assist you with a smooth ascent, but only when necessary. Consider the following:

>> **Maintain speed and pitch for a steady climb.** In most cases, you want to gently pull back on the yoke (shown in Figure 9-4) when you take off from the runway. After you're in the air, maintain that same pull to keep the pitch of the aircraft's nose at the same level. Going too high or too low can throw off the balance of horizontal and vertical speed, so try not to change pitch at all.

>> **Counteract slowing speed by pitching the nose down.** You shouldn't need to throttle up when you're in the air and pitching upwards. However, if you find your airspeed slowing (which you can see by looking at the airspeed indicator), try pitching the nose down with the stick — just a little — to level out. You still want to climb, but climbing too fast can cost you essential speed that you need to stay in the air.

Yoke                    Throttle

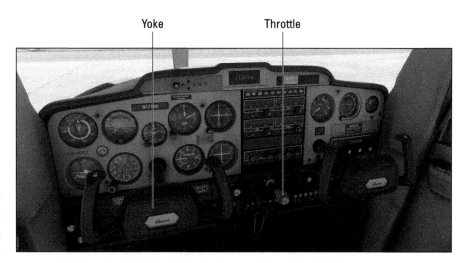

**FIGURE 9-4:**
Keep the throttle and yoke steady while you climb.

**REMEMBER**

Ensure that you continue climbing until well clear of any air traffic in the area. In most cases, you climb straight forward until you reach a specific altitude. This altitude may change, depending on the airport that you're leaving, but it's always around 5,500 feet for smaller aircraft or 10,000 for larger. Even then, your course may require you to simply keep flying straight ahead.

# Taking a turn

If you need to turn for your current flight plan, make those turns in very smooth, slow motions. Turning too fast can cause your aircraft to destabilize (see the section "Attending to alignment correction and vertical stabilization," earlier in this chapter) — which is bad news for you and any passengers onboard. Think of how smoothly a commercial aircraft turns when you're flying in one as a passenger. You want to mimic this type of movement as much as possible.

To make a smooth turn, start with a slow turn — by moving the stick or yoke gently right or left toward the direction you need to turn — then gradually increase the move until you reach the perfect yaw position. Also, keep these points in mind about turning your aircraft:

>> Always ensure that you have plenty of room for turns by making sure no obstacles are in your path.

>> Take the size of the aircraft into account (a larger aircraft takes longer to turn).

These precautions make the turning process much easier in the long run.

# Dealing with stalling

*Stalling* (a disruption causing a loss of lift) is one of the biggest risks that an aircraft faces when taking off and climbing. Stalling can cause a sudden — and catastrophic — loss of control. The wings of an aircraft are shaped so that air moves faster over the top of them than it does under the bottom. As the speed of moving air increases, the pressure decreases. Because the pressure on the top of the wings is lower, the higher pressure at the bottom pushes upward, lifting the aircraft.

A *stall* occurs when the balance of air pressure is upset. This situation most often occurs when either the angle of attack is too high, or the aircraft's speed is too low to maintain a smooth airflow across the top of the wings. The resulting pressure difference between the wing's top and the bottom surfaces may no longer generate the lift needed to keep the aircraft in the sky. When the airplane stalls, it essentially becomes like a rock in the air until it either recovers air flow balance or hits the ground.

# Inclination effects

Inclination is another important factor to consider when taking off and even when landing. *Inclination* is essentially the angle of the lines of Earth's magnetic field related to the surface of the Earth or an object. Inclination affects *lift*, which is an aerodynamic force that acts during takeoff (see Chapter 6). Your aircraft's inclination can cause an unbalance of the center of gravity and produce errors in turning and accelerating. While Flight Simulator doesn't simulate this, it's important to understand even with virtual flights.

If you find that you're experiencing too much acceleration or deceleration drift (keep an eye on your speedometer as shown in Figure 9-5), you may need to change the direction of your inclination. You don't really need to understand the technical definition and application of inclination if you want to fly, but you do need to have a good understanding of how to combat any issues it may cause.

**FIGURE 9-5:**
Keep an eye on your airspeed at any point in the flight.

Basically, think of inclination as the effect that gravity has on an object. When you're accelerating and moving upward in your aircraft, you need to be aware of the effects of inclination on the angle of your aircraft's climb (called the *angle of attack*). When you're landing, the inclination affects your airspeed and rate of descent. Keep these considerations in mind:

>> **Climbing (pitching up) too steeply:** Could cause gravity to pull on the aircraft too much, thus making it burn more fuel or even experience other issues, such as stalling. Counteract this situation by pitching slightly down.

>> **Pitching down too steeply:** Can make it difficult (or impossible) to slow down due to the force of gravity pulling on the aircraft. If your speed continues to climb when you're decelerating and trying to descend, you can adjust accordingly by pitching slightly up.

# Coming Home Again, Home Again

Suppose that you take off successfully (see the section "Making It Up into the Air," earlier in this chapter) and fly safely on course to your destination (which I talk about in Chapter 13). The time to land has arrived, and you need to find out about airport approach patterns, how to tweak your descent, and even how to maintain revolutions per minute (RPM) and airspeed in the approach patterns. Then, you can move on to the actual touchdown, which can be just as intricate to accomplish as takeoff, so you have to be careful.

## Navigating approach patterns

When you're preparing to land at an airport, you often need to take part in what pilots call *approach patterns* (the standard, often rectangular, paths for coordinating air traffic). These important circuits and related maneuvers allow you to prepare your aircraft for a perfect, smooth landing, while also keeping the airways around airports safe and clear for other traffic.

The approach patterns are important because they allow traffic to filter into the airport one way and out another. This coordination helps keep air traffic moving smoothly and safely separated from other traffic, something that's very important when dealing with massive airports where thousands of planes are taking off and landing every single day.

Depending on the layout of the airport where you're landing, as well as the wind speed and direction, you may be following a right-hand or left-hand traffic pattern. (Figure 9-6 shows both.) Essentially, the right or left direction refers to which side of the aircraft the airport appears on when you fly towards it to prepare for landing.

Regardless of the type of traffic pattern the airport uses, here are the main parts of approach patterns:

>> **Entry leg:** Your aircraft enters the main portion of the traffic pattern, which usually runs parallel to the intended runway. When you're preparing to transfer from the entry leg to the main portion of the pattern (either downwind or upwind), allow ample space around your aircraft that offers a clear view of the entire traffic pattern. This view helps ensure no chaos ensues when you enter the pattern.

>> **Downwind leg:** In this part of the pattern, you fly parallel to the runway and in the opposite direction of landing traffic. Simply follow the parallel path until you reach a distance great enough for a turn that you can use to enter a leg that runs perpendicular to the runway. This part of the pattern is referred to as the *base leg,* and you make your final turn to line up with the runway from it.

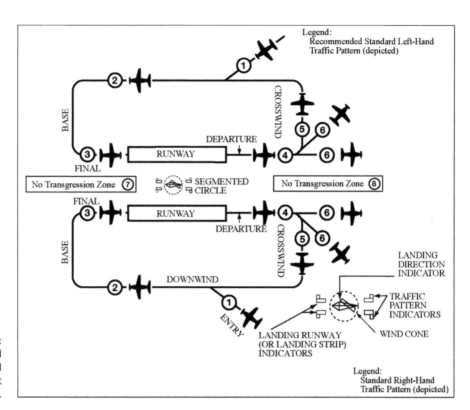

**FIGURE 9-6:**
Right- and left-hand airport patterns.

>> **Upwind leg:** Like the downwind leg, the upwind leg flies parallel to the runway, but in the same direction as the landing traffic. You may take an upwind leg in the traffic pattern when you plan to fly the entire rectangular pattern or are performing a go-around to allow for separation from other traffic.

>> **Crosswind leg:** The approach pattern may include a crosswind leg that you enter by turning 90 degrees in the direction of the runway from the upwind leg. This is the path running perpendicular to the runway and directly opposite the base leg (on the other end of the runway). You use the crosswind leg to enter the downwind leg of the approach pattern, again by turning 90 degrees.

>> **Base leg:** The part of the pattern where you fly perpendicular to the runway to the point where you can line up with the center of the airport's runway that you've been designated to land on. That's when you turn on the final leg.

Pay close attention to the position of your base leg because you want to have an ample amount of time on the final leg to pitch down and slow your aircraft before touchdown.

>> **Final leg:** In this part of the traffic pattern, you turn 90 degrees from the base leg to be lined up with the center of the runway. Then, you slow down and control your final descent to the ground. (See more about the actual landing in the section "Touching Down," later in this chapter.)

No matter which pattern direction you're using — right-hand or left-hand — the basic legs of the pattern are always the same.

## Tweaking your descent

When you reach the final leg of the approach pattern (see the preceding section), you must descend to the ground. Two important things to keep in mind at this point are your speed and rate of descent. Descending too fast without decreasing your speed means that

>> **You might hit the ground too hard.** This unfortunate situation can cause damage to your aircraft, which results in a Fail screen under normal circumstances.

>> **You might not brake in time after landing.** Insufficient time for braking can cause you to have to scrap the landing, take off, and complete the approaching pattern all over again.

You may find yourself having to tweak your descent on the spot by adjusting the throttle and your aircraft's pitch.

If you're not descending as quickly as you need to, simply adjust your pitch downward and reduce the throttle to increase your rate of descent. Likewise, if you're coming in too quickly, increase your pitch and add power to the throttle to slow down your descent. This game of balancing pitch and power may take some getting used to, but after some work, you'll get it down.

## Keeping an eye on RPM and airspeed

When you're descending for landing or taking off, pay attention to both the RPM and airspeed. The RPM is an indicator that your engines are working correctly and can maintain the speed that you need. Figure 9-7 shows the RPM indicator on an aircraft dashboard in Flight Simulator.

If your RPM speeds are high when landing, you can find yourself struggling to brake and slow the aircraft. Likewise, if the RPM is too low when taking off, you can struggle to lift off properly. Maintain a stable RPM by adjusting the throttle to ensure that takeoff and landing are both as smooth as possible.

FIGURE 9-7:
Keep an eye
on your RPM
indicator at all
times when
landing and
taking off.

*Airspeed* is the speed of an aircraft in relation to the air it's passing through. So, when you're dealing with airspeed, think of it as the aircraft's speedometer (refer to Figure 9-5). While you climb higher (and altitude increases), your airspeed becomes greater because air is *thinner* (it contains fewer gas molecules) and produces less resistance to your plane's forward movement. (See Chapter 6 for information about aerodynamic forces.)

When you're flying at lower altitudes (closer to the ground), the air provides more resistance, so your airspeed may be lower. In that situation, you increase power to the throttle to maintain a stable and proper airspeed at all times.

# Touching Down

When you need to put your plane's wheels on the ground again, you have to coordinate the activities outlined in the section "Coming Home Again, Home Again," earlier in this chapter: Navigating the airport approach, adjusting your rate and angle of descent, and balancing speed and power. Also, you need to consider what to do after you land your aircraft successfully on the airport's runway. There's a time to celebrate, but it isn't right after landing.

## Making a smooth landing

During the final leg of the airport's traffic pattern, all the factors described in the section "Coming Home Again, Home Again," earlier in this chapter, come into play. And just like your gentle and steady upward pitch helps you when taking off (see the section "Making It Up into the Air," earlier in this chapter), having a slight and stable downward pitch lets your aircraft almost glide onto the runway. See Figure 9-8. For some larger aircraft, maintaining this attitude can be more difficult, but practice makes it easier.

**FIGURE 9-8:**
Landing smoothly requires lining up your aircraft and keeping your pitch stable.

When descending, keep the nose of your aircraft from dipping too low because pitching downward increases your speed and makes leveling out the aircraft more difficult. Instead, go for a level descent that sees the entirety of your aircraft moving down towards the runway at the same time, ensuring that you can touch down smoothly without causing damage to your aircraft. To manage this level descent, follow these steps:

1. **Pitch forward (push the yoke forward) to begin the decent.**

2. **Keep an eye on the vertical speed indicator to make sure you're not descending too quickly.**

3. **Throttle down your engines as you descend to avoid excessive speed.**

4. **Press the correct key/button or use the correct lever/button in cockpit view to get your landing gear out.**

   If your aircraft can't stow the landing gear, you don't have to worry about this step.

5. **Apply flaps (if needed) to bleed off excess speed and maintain lift.**

6. **Pitch the aircraft's nose up just a little by pulling back on the yoke/stick before touching down.**

   The back wheels have the most weight on them and need to touch down first.

**TIP**

After touching down, immediately apply the brakes to slow down your aircraft. You're probably still traveling fast, and you need to slow down quickly without making the effect too jarring on your copilot or any passengers that you might have. To slow without jarring, you can gradually apply the breaks or reverser if your aircraft is equipped with one.

# Getting instructions for your next moves

If you follow the steps in the preceding section, you've successfully landed your aircraft. Great job. But don't start celebrating yet. After all, you're still on the runway.

After you touch down and slow down your aircraft, you need to taxi off the runway so that the next aircraft can land. Reach out to ATC and get taxi instructions. Oftentimes, the instructions lead you to a gate where you can pull in and complete the flight (as shown in Figure 9-9). If you're flying a smaller aircraft, you may be directed to personal hangers where you can stash your aircraft or prepare for the next flight. Check out Chapter 11 for the lowdown on communicating with ATC.

**FIGURE 9-9:** Celebrate after you reach your gate.

Either way, get those instructions from ATC and then get off the runway as quickly as possible to avoid any kind of buildup of traffic, which could cause chaos in the airport's current traffic pattern.

# 3

# Airport Operations

**IN THIS PART . . .**

Examine airports and their components, navigate arrival and departure locations, and appreciate the detail of handcrafted airports in Microsoft Flight Simulator 2020.

Find out how to communicate with air traffic control (ATC), understand all that radio chatter, and work through the sequence of instructions from takeoff to landing.

# Chapter **10**

# Knowing Your Way Around the Airport

n real life, almost every flight starts and ends at an airport. And so when a pilot files a flight plan with air traffic control (ATC), that plan includes departure and arrival airports. Many aspects of the journey depend on those two locations. Real-world pilots understand the characteristics — such as runway length and direction, availability of fuel, and so on — of the chosen airports and whether those characteristics are compatible with the aircraft they're flying and the duration of their flight. For example, pilots need to know that the runway at the arrival airport is long enough to accommodate the landing requirements of the plane and that they can refuel at the arrival airport if they want to fly to another destination or back to the departure airport.

You don't have the same obligation to understand airport and aircraft compatibility if you're playing Microsoft Flight Simulator 2020, as compared to actually flying the non-virtual skies. You can plop your plane in the air and fly to your heart's content without ever worrying about coming down. However, if you're interested in the simulator aspects of the game, you need to know how to choose your beginning and ending airports and how to get around those airports. Many people are familiar with the terminals of their local airports, but they give little thought to the airport's runways, taxiways, jetways, and other ways.

In this chapter, you can find out about the ways (runways, taxiways, and so on) that make up the physical aspects of an airport and how planes navigate this structure. You can also get a bit of advice about choosing your departure and arrival airports, including a list of the *handcrafted airports*, which are airports created by Asobo Studios to represent a more realistic airport experience than the AI-created airports that make up the majority of facilities you'll find in the simulator. Flight Simulator provides these handcrafted airports in case you're interested in that real-world feel.

# Finding the Runway and Other Ways

The commercial airports that many of us know are sprawling complexes. Multiple buildings, roads, depots, and parking areas make up a typical airport (a portion of one is shown in Figure 10-1). However, not every *aerodrome* (a facility for accommodating aircraft) requires such a massive investment in manpower and materials.

**FIGURE 10-1:** An airliner parked at a gate.

The International Civil Aviation Organization (ICAO) defines an aerodrome as

> "A defined area on land or water (including any buildings, installations, and equipment) intended to be used either wholly or in part for the arrival, departure, and movement of aircraft."

So, any patch of land or water that regularly sees air traffic can be an aerodrome.

But are all aerodromes airports? No! The ICAO doesn't have a specific definition for what makes an aerodrome an airport. Confusingly, the United States uses the term *landing area* rather than *aerodrome*, and U.S. law defines an airport as "a landing area used regularly by aircraft for receiving or discharging passengers or cargo."

**REMEMBER**

At least in the U.S., the difference between an airport and a landing area is that the former sees regular traffic. So, given the definition of an airport (at least, in the United States), you can begin to look at the components that regular traffic commonly uses.

## Admiring the apron (or parking or stands)

An airport *apron* consists of anywhere in an airport where planes are parked. Sometimes, the term is used interchangeably with *stand, tarmac,* or *ramp.* However, the official ICAO terminology is *apron.* You can basically think of this apron as anywhere that airplanes go within the airport property that isn't the taxiway or runway.

In addition to the apron, *parking* is a general term used to designate anywhere that an aircraft might be parked. Because the ICAO offers no official definition of what areas of the airport must be designated as parking, the term is interchangeably used to refer to parts of the apron or stands. Many times, pilots refer to *parking* as the location where they can power down and possibly store an aircraft. A hangar is the best illustration of an aircraft parking location.

Also, an aircraft *stand* is anywhere on the apron that's designated for the parking of aircraft. An aircraft can be parked at a stand for loading and unloading cargo or passengers, or for performing maintenance or refueling. A parking spot is usually designated a stand when it's located away from a terminal gate. A *terminal gate* is the area where passengers board their designated aircraft and depart on their flights. Gates generally have waiting areas where passengers can gather to await seat assignments (if they don't already have one) and listen for their gate numbers to be called.

## Recognizing a runway

For a location to qualify as an aerodrome, it needs to have a runway. And most commercial airports have two or more *runways,* the airport components where the magic of flight begins and ends. They're extended, rectangular, road-like areas that aircraft use to gain enough speed to obtain liftoff and to slow down and brake when they land. Figure 10-2 shows a plane on the runway.

FIGURE 10-2:
All flights
(ideally) begin
and end on the
runway.

You can make a runway out of any substance that can be compacted enough to withstand the weight of a landing aircraft and can enable that aircraft to safely come to a stop. Each runway has a designation, which may have two parts:

» **Magnetic direction:** Traditionally, a runway is named for its magnetic direction rounded to the nearest 10 degrees, with the last digit truncated.

» **Orientation within the airport:** When an airport has more than one runway, part of the designation describes the runway's relative position (as in left or right).

So, for example, the designation *Runway 17L* lets pilots know that they'll take off and land pointed toward heading 170 degrees on (typically) the leftmost (L) runway.

REMEMBER

Because aircraft need to take off and land into the wind to ease liftoffs and landings, each runway has two designations. The designation being used indicates which direction aircraft are taking off and landing in for the day. So, when the wind is blowing in a southerly direction (toward 180 degrees), the Runway 17L label (seen when approaching from the north) becomes a Runway 35R label because airplanes approach from a southerly direction in order to land into the wind.

TIP

Any pilots, but beginning pilots especially, should make themselves aware of runway length. The longer a runway is, the more time you have to abort or correct issues before taking flight, or to slow to a reasonable speed for navigating the taxiways when landing. The rule tends to be that the larger and heavier an aircraft is, the more runway it needs to take off or land. Don't try to land your Airbus 320 on an Alaskan bush airstrip.

# Traveling the taxiways

*Taxiways* are designated routes for aircraft movement on the ground at an airport. These roadways, as shown in Figure 10-3, connect aprons with hangars, runways, terminals, and other airport facilities. Navigating the taxiways may be the most confusing aspect of airport operations for new pilots. Each taxiway has its own designation, and pilots must follow a prescribed route (provided by ATC) along the taxiways to and from the runway. Failure to follow this route can lead to a crash.

Taxiway     Apron     Hangar

**FIGURE 10-3:** Taxiway navigation is one of the big challenges of airport operations.

**TIP**

Luckily, Flight Simulator includes a setting (in the Assistance options described in Chapter 6) that you can use to activate an onscreen waypoint. This *waypoint,* a series of blue arrows, shows which way pilots need to taxi. Even experienced pilots can benefit from the helpful guide because anyone can find trying to read the tiny signs marking taxiway routes frustrating.

# Identifying a terminal

A *terminal* is an airport building where passengers deplane or wait for boarding, and where cargo is stored for loading and unloading. In some airports, especially regional ones, passengers may board and deplane outside of the terminal. Although this situation is somewhat rare in the United States, it's relatively common in other countries. Some of the largest buildings in the world (by usable floor area) are airport terminals because they must accommodate the massive influxes of passengers and cargo that come with plane landings.

Larger airport terminals are designed to accommodate dozens of aircraft at a time. Figure 10-4 shows a large terminal building with airplanes at the terminal's gates (see the following section for more info on gates). Airliners tend to connect to a terminal via a large movable bridge called a *jetway.* However, smaller airplanes require passengers to board and deplane straight from the apron.

FIGURE 10-4:
Terminals
come in all
shapes and
sizes.

## Getting on at the gate

Each passenger flight is assigned a gate. *Gates* typically have an interior waiting area for passengers, and each gate is serviced by one or more attendants from the airline to which the gate is assigned. When an aircraft is prepared for boarding, passengers make their way through the gate and onto the plane via a jetway or by passing through an exterior door and entering from the apron.

## Tracking with the tower

An airport *tower* is the building where air traffic controllers work to guide the movement of aircraft both on the ground and in the surrounding airspace. A tower may have sensors such as radar installed on it, which it uses to track aircraft. Generally, the tower is the tallest building in an airport complex. The tower's height provides controllers with a good visual reference to the layout of the airport.

# What You Can Do at Airports

Because airports serve as a hub of air travel, most pilots spend a lot of time rolling along the taxiways of Flight Simulator. Unfortunately, the Flight Simulator airports don't offer a deeply authentic simulation of how these facilities work in real life.

The most noticeable aspect of real airports that's missing in the game is foot traf-fic. Aside from the non-player characters (NPCs) that drive the ground services vehicles, airports are barren, like the lifeless scene shown in Figure 10-5. So, you have to use your imagination to fill in the thousands of passengers, airline staff, and airport personnel that would normally inhabit the area.

**FIGURE 10-5:**
Some players find Flight Simulator's airport simula-tions lacking in humans.

The lack of passenger simulation has a ripple effect throughout the game. Of course, you can add the weight of passengers to an airliner, but maybe you want to see them board the plane and have that feeling of being responsible for all the passengers on a fully booked airliner. That said, you as a virtual pilot can do a few things at airports to help give you the illusion of the real thing. You can

>> **Interact with gates and ground services.** When a passenger plane parks at a gate, pilots can ask ground services to attach the jetway, bring in baggage and catering, and more. You make these requests by using your radio. Although these activities don't directly influence a flight, they do enhance the sim experience.

>> **Follow ATCs taxi and takeoff instructions.** The air traffic control in the Flight Simulator game gives you taxiing and takeoff instructions, just like the real thing does when directing a real plane. Following the correct route — rather than just heading straight for the runway — adds to the game's challenge. And it also shows you why it sometimes takes so long to take off after leaving the gate in real life.

# Identifying Compatible Airports

Flight Simulator virtual pilots have a myriad of details to consider when choosing arrival and departure locations. Unlike in real life, these virtual pilots aren't limited by an airline telling them where to fly, and the Federal Aviation Administration (FAA) doesn't bat an eye if they try to land a 747 on a tiny desert airstrip or on a mountain top (see Figure 10-6).

**FIGURE 10-6:** Airports can be tiny strips on tall mountains or giant international hubs.

However, if you want an authentic flight experience, consider aspects of your target airports in conjunction with your skill and your aircraft's capabilities:

» **Range:** Does your aircraft have the fuel stores to make it from your departure airport to its arrival location? You can find out your plane's range — when you have a full tank of gas — by checking out the range circle on the World Map screen.

» **Ability:** Are you skilled enough to take off and land from the departure and arrival locations? Remember that some airports are more challenging than others for taking off and landing. For example, Juancho E. Yrausquin Airport has a sharp dropoff on either end of the runway.

» **Facilities:** Can that tiny arrival airstrip handle a taxing A320, or should you try flying an aircraft that's a bit smaller? Take the time to find out about the arrival airport's runway length and match your plane to it.

>> **Endurance:** Are you up for a five-hour flight (if you're not increasing the sim speed)? Recognize that you may need to pick a closer destination if you want to complete your flight from takeoff to landing.

Keeping these points in mind can prevent many an aborted flight. To select an airport for takeoff and landing in Flight Simulator, use the tools on the World Map screen.

## Choosing a departure location

Players have more leeway when it comes to choosing a departure airport, as compared to a destination (discussed in the following section). Taking off is much easier than landing is. So, the skies are the limit (pun intended) when it comes to picking your origin point for even intermediate pilots. Beginners might want to stick with established, well-maintained airports (see Figure 10-7) while they take practice flights to gain experience. But as long as you have enough runway length for your airplane, anywhere makes for a good departure.

FIGURE 10-7:
Pilots can successfully take off, even on a smaller airstrip.

## Choosing an arrival location

Choosing an arrival location is much more complicated than selecting your airport of departure (see the preceding section). Landing is a challenge under ideal circumstances and can become nearly impossible, depending on the airport. Figure 10-8 shows a rural airport that has an unpaved runway, which not all types of aircraft can land on.

FIGURE 10-8:
Landing on concrete is very different than bouncing around a dirt airstrip.

Beginner virtual pilots should stick to facilities that have long, paved runways and navigation aids such as

>> **Instrument Landing System (ILS):** A precision landing aid that uses a radio navigation system to provide short-range guidance to aircraft via two directional radio signals, the localizer and the glideslope.

>> **Approach Lighting System (ALS):** A lighting system that consists of a series of lightbars or strobe lights that extend outward from the runway. It enables pilots to visually identify the runway and align their aircraft properly.

>> **Precision Approach Path Indicator (PAPI):** A series of lights that serves as a visual aid to help pilots use the correct angle of approach to the runway.

While you gain more experience, landing at less hospitable airports can give you a great test of your abilities. Those who stick with Flight Simulator long enough can touch down on runways that are little more than paths scratched into some compacted dirt.

# Is Your Chosen Airport the Real Deal?

Crafting the world presented in Flight Simulator is a remarkable accomplishment, but it's far from a 1:1 recreation of the Earth and its airports. Asobo Games utilized satellite imagery and topographical data to procedurally recreate our planet. Unfortunately, most locations are still lacking when it comes to detail. Additionally, the algorithm that the studio used to fill out the map sometimes makes some questionable decisions about where to place trees, houses, roads, and buildings. And so, you may be wondering how close the airports in the game come to representing the real deal.

You can find two types of airports in Flight Simulator:

» **Procedurally generated:** Created by algorithms to mixed results, some computer-generated airports are decent facsimiles of the real thing — but others just aren't.

» **Handcrafted:** Because the AI-generated results aren't perfect, Asobo Studios supplements them with handcrafted airports that are much truer to life. Figure 10-9 shows the handcrafted John F. Kennedy International Airport in New York City.

FIGURE 10-9:
Asobo
Studios has
handcrafted
some of the
most iconic
airports in the
world.

The following tables list the handcrafted airports you can find in the game as of this writing. Table 10-1 gives you all the airports that come handcrafted in the Standard Edition of Flight Simulator. Table 10-2 shows what handcrafted airports are added onto the Standard Edition list if you have the Deluxe Edition. And if you have the Premium Edition, you get all those airports, plus the ones listed in Table 10-3. Get all the handcrafted airports in Table 10-4 if you download these free updates.

**REMEMBER**

Asobo Studios adds a handful of handcrafted airports in almost every major update, so even if you don't see your favorite in these tables, keep an eye out for it in updates to your version of Flight Simulator.

**TABLE 10-1**     ## Standard Edition Handcrafted Airports

| ICAO Code | Airport Name | Location |
|-----------|--------------|----------|
| CAMA | Bugalaga Airstrip | Indonesia |
| CYTZ | Billy Bishop Toronto City | Ontario, Canada |
| CZST | Stewart | British Columbia, Canada |
| EIDL | Donegal | Ireland |
| HUEN | Entebbe | Uganda |
| KASE | Aspen/Pitkin County | Colorado, USA |
| KEB | Nanwalek | Alaska, USA |
| KJFK | John F. Kennedy International | New York, USA |
| KLAX | Los Angeles | California, USA |
| KMCO | Orlando | Florida, USA |
| KSEA | Seattle–Tacoma | Washington, USA |
| KSEZ | Sedona | Arizona, USA |
| KTEX | Telluride Regional | Colorado, USA |
| LFLJ | Courchevel Altiport | France |
| LFPG | Paris Charles de Gaulle | France |
| LOWI | Innsbruck | Austria |
| LPMA | Cristiano Ronaldo (Madeira) International | Portugal |
| LXGB | Gibraltar | Gibraltar (U.K. territory) |
| MHTG | Toncontin International | Honduras |
| MRSN | Sirena Aerodrome | Costa Rica |
| NZQN | Queenstown | New Zealand |
| RJTT | Haneda | Japan |

| ICAO Code | Airport Name | Location |
| --- | --- | --- |
| SEQM | Mariscal Sucre International | Ecuador |
| SGBL | Rio de Janeiro | Brazil |
| SPGL | Chagual | Peru |
| TFFJ | Gustaf III Airport | Saint Barthélemy (French territory) |
| TNCS | Juancho E. Yrausquin | Dutch Saba |
| VNLK | Tenzing-Hillary | Nepal |
| VQPR | Paro International | Bhutan |
| YSSY | Sydney | New South Wales, Australia |

**TABLE 10-2**    **Deluxe Edition Handcrafted Airports**

| ICAO Code | Airport Name | Location |
| --- | --- | --- |
| EHAM | Amsterdam Schiphol | The Netherlands |
| FACT | Cape Town | South Africa |
| HECA | Cairo | Egypt |
| KORD | O'Hare International | Illinois, USA |
| LEMD | Madrid–Barajas | Spain |

**TABLE 10-3**    **Premium Edition Handcrafted Airports**

| ICAO Code | Airport Name | Location |
| --- | --- | --- |
| EDDF | Frankfurt | Germany |
| EGLL | London Heathrow | U.K. |
| KDEN | Denver | Colorado, USA |
| KSFO | San Francisco | California, USA |
| OMDB | Dubai | UAE |

TABLE 10-4 # Handcrafted Airports by Update

| Update | ICAO Code | Airport Name | Location |
|---|---|---|---|
| World Update 1 | PAFR | Bryant Army Airfield Heliport | Alaska, USA |
| | RJCK | Kushiro | Japan |
| | RJFU | Nagasaki | Japan |
| | RJTH | Hachijojima | Japan |
| | RJX8 | Suwanosejima | Japan |
| | ROKR | Kerama | Japan |
| | RORS | Shimojisjima | Japan |
| World Update 2 | C53 | Lower Loon Creek | Idaho, USA |
| | KATL | Atlanta International | Georgia, USA |
| | KDFW | Dallas/Fort Worth | Texas, USA |
| | KFHR | Friday Harbor | Washington, USA |
| | KSWF | New York Stewart | New York, USA |
| World Update 3 | EGCB | Manchester–Barton | U.K. |
| | EGGP | Liverpool | U.K. |
| | EGHC | Land's End | U.K. |
| | EGOU | Outer Skerries | U.K. |
| | EGPR | Barra | U.K. |
| World Update 4 | EHRD | Rotterdam The Hague | The Netherlands |
| | LFHM | Megève Airport | France |
| | LFMN | Nice Côte d'Azur | France |
| World Update 5 | BIIS | Isafjordur | Iceland |
| | EFVA | Vaasa | Finland |
| | EKRN | Bornholm | Denmark |
| | ENSB | Svalbard | Norway |
| | ESSA | Stockholm–Arlanda | Sweden |
| World Update 6 | EDDS | Stuttgart | Germany |
| | EDHL | Lübeck | Germany |
| | EDXH | Heliogoland | Germany |

| Update | ICAO Code | Airport Name | Location |
|---|---|---|---|
| | LOWK | Klagenfurt | Austria |
| | LSZR | St. Gallen–Altenrhein | Switzerland |
| Sim Update 7 (Game of the Year) | EDDP | Leipzig/Halle Airport | Germany |
| | EDJA | Allgäu Airport Memmingen | Germany |
| | EDVK | Kassel Airport | Germany |
| | KCOF | Patrick Space Force Base | Florida, USA |
| | KNKX | Marine Corps Air Station Miramar | California, USA |
| | LSZA | Lugano Airport | Switzerland |
| | LSZH | Zurish Airport | Switzerland |
| | LSZO | Luzern–Beromunster Airport | Switzerland |

# Chapter **11**

# Talking Your Way Into (and Through) the Air

The logistics of managing air traffic are complicated, and preventing accidents requires an extreme amount of vigilance. Managing the safe and efficient flow of automobile traffic is tough enough, and those vehicles move in only two dimensions. Because you can't just mark travel lanes on the airway and hang stoplights in the air, controlling air traffic is significantly more complicated and requires dedicated monitoring.

In Microsoft Flight Simulator 2020, you get a taste of the role that the air traffic control (ATC) service plays in ensuring that thousands of flights per day have safe journeys. From the time you turn on your plane's engines and prepare for takeoff until you land and power down, you listen to and follow instructions from the ATC ground-based watchguards called air traffic controllers.

What exactly does ATC do, though? The ATC service directs pilots and their aircraft while they navigate the runways and taxiways of an airport, and it also governs a section of controlled airspace. When you're a passenger on a private or commercial flight, you have zero contact with the influential individuals in the ATC service who monitor and manage air traffic. But Flight Simulator gives you a great way to get acquainted with them and discover even more about airport operations. In this chapter, you find out how to communicate with ATC, what functions the ATC window provides, and the features and limitations of Flight Simulator's ATC system.

# Engaging with ATC

Air traffic control (ATC) is a service provided by ground-based air traffic controllers (also abbreviated ATCs) who operate from a control tower, as shown in Figure 11-1. ATC's main purpose is to organize air traffic, manage the flow, and prevent collisions. It also provides information — typically in the form of Automatic Terminal Information Service (ATIS) transmissions — that tells you the current temperature, altimeter, and airport information.

**FIGURE 11-1**
A typical air traffic control tower.

## Communicating continuously with ATC

Flights begin and end with a transmission to ATC. As the pilot in command, you operate under the authority of one controller or another throughout your journey. Flight Simulator features a relatively rudimentary (but serviceable) facsimile of what it's like to communicate with ATC that gives players a taste of how the interactions work in real life. You may find a few quirks to the ATC system that's currently implemented in the game; these show the limitations of the system.

Flight Simulator is an impressive simulation game, but it can't quite provide a fully authentic experience. In the game, you handle communications with ATC through a window (shown in Figure 11-2) that presents multiple-choice selections. The choices prompt you to select one of the local communication channels and present the currently available actions for that channel.

## Finding options for an authentic ATC experience

Suppose that you want to have an experience communicating with ATC that's as authentic as possible. In that case, you can tune into each channel, or station, by using your plane's radio panel. Keep in mind that how well each radio panel is modeled in Flight Simulator depends on the plane you're flying. Some radios are close to a one-to-one comparison with the real-life aircrafts, but others are actually barely functional. Still, the novelty for most people wears off very quickly when the extra effort required becomes apparent.

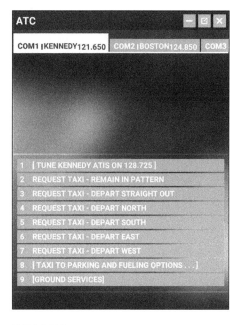

**FIGURE 11-2:**
The ATC window in Flight Simulator.

TECHNICAL STUFF

Because of the limits of the in-game ATC system (such as being limited to canned responses), many pilots who are serious about getting an authentic simulation turn to mods. If you want to get the full ATC experience, third-party services such as VATSIM can connect pilots with a network of users roleplaying as ATC. (VATSIM stands for the Virtual Air Traffic Simulation Network, and you can find and join it for free online at www.vatsim.net.)

# Observing the Rules while Communicating with ATC

Communicating while ATC guides you through taxi, takeoff, and into the air doesn't mean you're done talking to them. You continue keeping in close contact with ATC throughout your flight. Those pilots who use Instrument Flight Rules (IFR) flight plans must worry about altitude clearances and handoffs, while those flying by using Visual Flight Rules (VFR) flight plans need to prepare for airspace clearances and *flight following* (which happens when ATC follows your flight via radar and provides location services). Differences in ATC communications correspond to the two sets of flight rules:

>> **IFR:** Your successful IFR flight relies on talking with ATC all through the flight. Maintaining this communication while your flight progresses is extremely important. Pay attention to the different handoffs and make sure to change to any new communication frequencies that ATC gives you.

REMEMBER

Many times, IFR flight plans can take you through clouds or other areas that have low visibility. That means you're going to rely very heavily on the instruments you have in front of you in the cockpit, along with instructions from ATC, to avoid other planes and obstacles along your route.

>> **VFR:** With VFR flight plans, you rely somewhat on instruments, but you rely more on the landmarks and other features that you can see from the cockpit. You can fly towards your heading by using landmarks that you recognize, as well as roadways and other ground references that you see around you. During VFR flight, a lot of the contact that you make with ATC has to do with permissions for entering airspaces along your route and ensuring you aren't going anywhere you shouldn't.

Talking with ATC can take some getting used to, especially while you work to acquaint yourself with VFR and IFR rules. Overall, though, the way you talk to ATC is similar in both sets of flight rules, and a lot of the tuning and confirmations carry over between them. But you do have additional options when flying with IFR, compared to VFR; for example, you can request altitude changes, ask for direction (heading) changes, and make other shifts, such as changing landing runways, to your flight plan. ATC needs to approve all such changes to avoid any in-air collisions or conflicts with your flight plan down the line.

# Working through an ATC Communications Sequence

REMEMBER

Keep in mind that the ATC system in the game works like the dialog system from a role-playing game (RPG), such as Fallout or Elder Scrolls, which means that you're choosing from a pre-written list of options. Likewise, the ATC in Flight Simulator expects you to know the proper sequence of calling in, getting clearances, and staying in contact throughout your flight. However, you do this communicating by selecting a particular dialog source, not by actually speaking the words yourself.

In Flight Simulator, you make selections from a radio panel, as shown in Figure 11-3, to communicate with ATC. You can also use this panel to manually tune channels, but dialog is handled by way of the ATC/Radio window.

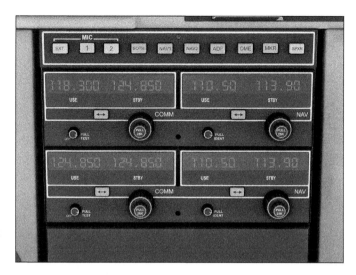

FIGURE 11-3:
A standard
radio panel.

In the following sections, I take you through an example of what ATC management and communications look like during an average flight in Flight Simulator. The example flight uses a Lockheed P-38 Lightning aircraft (available via the Marketplace, which you can read about in Chapter 3) that has callsign N177AB.

## Obtaining ATIS frequencies and info

As soon as pilots power up their aircraft, they tune their radio into the local Automatic Terminal Information Service (ATIS) frequency to get the information broadcast for the airport. You can easily access ATIS info when playing Flight Simulator because ATIS is always on the default list of radio channels on the ATC panel.

Suppose that you start a flight at Muhammad Ali International Airport (formerly Standiford Field) (ICAO: KSDF) in Louisville, Kentucky. When you power on your radio, you see the following options for communication on your ATC panel:

1. Tune Ground on 121.700

2. Tune Standiford ATIS on 118.720

3. Tune Clearance on 126.100

4. Ground Services

Selecting the second option tunes into the local ATIS channel, and you immediately hear its broadcast, which gives you the following info:

>> **The airfield:** Where ATIS is broadcasting from; in this case, it's the Muhammad Ali International Airport (KSDF).

>> **The current time:** Typically given in Zulu time, also known as Universal Time Coordinated (UTC).

>> **Active runways:** Including which runways are in use for both arrivals and departures.

>> **Local conditions:** Including

- Wind speed and direction

- Current visibility distance and cloud cover

- Temperature

- Altimeter setting

>> **Other relevant information:** Such as bird activity and other special notes that affect flight conditions

TIP

The altimeter setting is the biggest item to note when listening to ATIS in Flight Simulator. By default, your altimeter is set to the standard of 29.92 inches, which isn't always correct. Setting the altimeter according to the ATIS broadcast ensures that your cockpit instrumentation gives you the proper readings.

## Getting departure approval

Predictably, the ground ATC service handles all aircraft operations on the ground, such as taxiing, parking, and traffic control. In Flight Simulator, your flight begins with a call to ground ATC or the control tower, depending on whether you're flying VFR or IFR (see the section "Observing the Rules while Communicating with ATC," earlier in this chapter, for more).

For a VFR flight, to get to the runway to take off, you must get taxi instructions from Ground:

> **You:** Ground, Lockheed N177AB request taxi for takeoff, departing (*fill in the direction you intend to fly after you take off*).

For an IFR flight, the communications are a bit different. Instead of calling Ground first, you contact the control tower:

**You:** Clearance Delivery, Lockheed N177AB IFR to (*destination*), ready to copy.

**Tower:** Lockheed N177AB, is cleared to (*destination*) airport as filed. Takeoff runway (*departure runway*), climb and maintain (*altitude*). Departure frequency is (*frequency*), squawk (*transponder code*).

**You:** (*Read back departure details to confirm.*)

**Tower:** Lockheed N177AB, readback is correct. Contact Ground on 121.7 when ready to taxi. Good day.

# Receiving and following taxi instructions

Following the taxi instructions without assistance is one of the most challenging tasks that a pilot faces on the ground. Figure 11-4 shows a diagram of the taxiways and runways from this chapter's example departure airport (the Muhammad Ali International Airport).

For VFR flights, Ground ATC relays taxi instructions as part of departure approval. For IFR flights, pilots make a separate call to Ground ATC after receiving departure approval from the tower and request taxi instructions.

Regardless of which type of flight rules you're following, the taxi instructions come in the same format:

**Ground:** Lockheed N177AB taxi to and hold short of runway 17R via taxiway M cross runway 17L E A cross runway 17R. Contact tower on (*frequency*) when ready.

**You:** (*Read back taxi instructions to confirm.*)

Beginning at the gate or ramp where the aircraft is sitting and breaking down the above taxi instructions, you follow these steps to reach the departure runway:

1. **Take taxiway M to runway 17L.**

2. **Follow taxiway M across runway 17L until you reach taxiway E.**

3. **Turn onto taxiway E and continue until you reach taxiway A.**

4. **Turn onto taxiway A and follow it to runway 17R.**

5. **Cross runway 17R and stay on taxiway A until you reach the last turn onto runway 17R.**

6. **Hold short (stop right before entering the runway) and contact the tower for departure.**

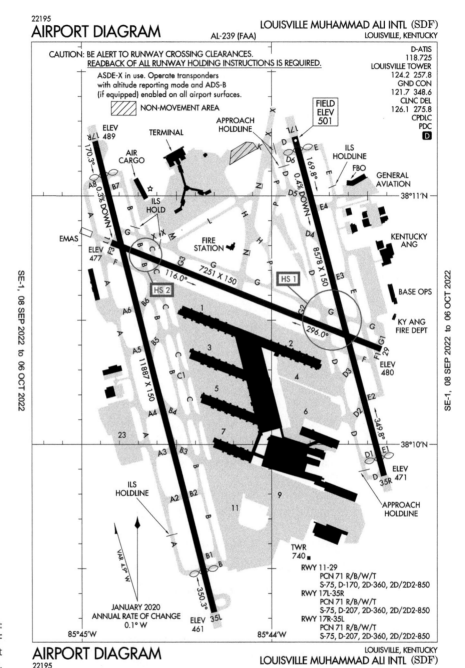

FIGURE 11-4:
The KSDF
airport
diagram.

TIP

So how are you supposed to know where all these taxiways are and which way to turn? Flight Simulator offers you some help; you can

>> **Turn on the guideline that directs your taxiing path via the AI assistance panel.**

>> **Try to read the little signs on the ground that mark each taxiway.** The information on these signs tells you the runway numbers and taxiway letters. Figure 11-5 shows a sign that designates taxiway C in the game.

>> **Use an airport diagram that you find by visiting the FAA website.** The diagram plainly maps out each taxiway, but diagrams aren't accurate for every airport.

FIGURE 11-5:
Taxiways are designated by these little signs.

WARNING

One of the quirks of Flight Simulator is that the only airports recreated with high accuracy are the handcrafted ones. The procedurally generated ones, such as Muhammad Ali International Airport, frequently have discrepancies, such as mislabeled taxiways.

## Getting the go-ahead for takeoff

After you make it to the runway (the preceding section helps you get there), you just need to make one more call, and then it's time to head off into the wild blue yonder. Change over to the tower frequency on your radio panel and ask for permission to take off.

You get a slight variation on the conversation with the tower, depending on the kind of flight plan you choose:

>> For VFR:

   **You:** Louisville Tower, Lockheed N177AB at runway 17R ready for departure, departing (*departure direction*).

   **Tower:** Lockheed N177AB, altimeter 29.92, wind 285 at 5, departing (*departure direction*) approved. Cleared for takeoff runway 17R.

>> For IFR:

   **You:** Louisville Tower, Lockheed N177AB ready for departure, runway 17R, IFR to (*destination*).

   **Tower:** Lockheed N177AB, altimeter 29.92, wind 285 at 5. Cleared for takeoff runway 17R.

For either type of flight plan, you can proceed onto the runway, accelerate, and take to the air when you reach the right speed. Chapter 3 offers simple takeoff instructions.

## Keeping contact with ATC while in the air

After you take off from the departure airport, your aircraft remains under the watchful eye of the same ATC while it stays within that airport's airspace. And ATC lets you know when you're leaving its airspace. When you leave an ATC's airspace, one of two things can result:

>> **If you're flying an IFR flight plan:** ATC hands you off to another ATC frequency for altitude clearances and other changes. When you use an IFR flight plan, you're basically flying using the instruments on your plane, as well as those that ATC has access to. Because of that, you need to rely heavily on the information that ATC relays to you. This information can include altitude and direction changes while ATC works to keep you clear of other aircraft.

   On an IFR flight, you can request directions to the waypoints in your plan by selecting Request Vector To Next Waypoint from the ATC menu. When you select this option, you reach out to ATC, and they respond with which direction to turn, at what heading to point your plane, and even any altitude changes you might need to make.

>> **If you have a VFR flight:** Things remain much the same as with IFR. But instead of getting a vector to a waypoint, you can request a position readout. When you make the request, ATC gives you your position relative to a landmark. For example, "N177AB is 7 miles northwest of Bowman Field."

For either IFR or VFR flight plans, ATC may, at times, give you a *squawk code* that identifies your aircraft. You set your transponder to the squawk code frequency (by entering it into the transponder, the method of which differs by plane model), and ATC uses this frequency to keep track of you and see exactly which airplane you are on their radar screen. Make sure to pay attention to any changes to that squawk code and initiate them as soon as possible.

ATC notifies you of any airspace changes when your plane registers to them. For example, when you leave the airspace of the departure airport in this chapter's example, here's what talking to ATC looks like:

> **Tower:** Lockheed N177AB, you are leaving my airspace, frequency change approved.

> **You:** Louisville Tower, Lockheed N177AB, frequency change.

At that point, you see another option appear in your ATC menu: Tune Approach On (*Frequency*). Set your communications channel to the given frequency or choose this option from the ATC window. Continue your flight and ATC conversations on this frequency to keep in the loop on everything.

## Acquiring approach and landing instructions

When you approach your destination airport, you need to start talking to ATC heavily. Figure 11-6 shows the ATC window appears when your flight is on approach to the airport in Louisville. Follow these steps to work with ATC to get yourself safely on the ground:

1. **Tune into the frequency of the airport that you want to speak with by selecting the Nearest Airport List option from the ATC menu and then confirm your choice.**

   If you're flying IFR, you need to stick to your flight plan, so make sure to choose the airport where you planned to land.

2. **With the airport selected, connect to the tower in that area with the ATC window.**

3. **Request a Full Stop Landing by confirming the option in the ATC window.**

   You request landing clearance, provide details on how far away you are from the airport, and specify from which direction you're coming to the airport.

The ATC responds with details about your approach and landing clearance. These details often include the direction you need to travel in relationship to the runway (crosswind, downwind, and so on). The ATC response also provides you with the wind direction, speed, and which runway you'll be landing on.

4. **After receiving your instructions, make sure you acknowledge them (via a readback of instructions) with the ATC before you proceed.**

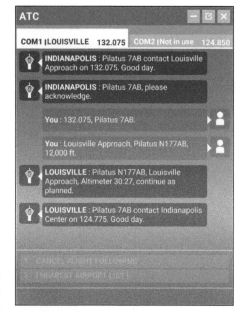

**FIGURE 11-6:**
Check in with ATC when on approach for landing.

After you land on the ground, ATC provides you with details on when to exit the runway and/or which taxiway to take for exiting. After you exit the runway, ATC hands you off to Ground control, which requires you to tune to the new frequency for instructions on where to go. If you're landing at Muhammad Ali International Airport, for example, that interaction may look like this:

**Tower:** Lockheed N177AB, exit runway when able.

**Tower:** Lockheed N177AB, contact ground on 128.8

You then tune your communications channel to 128.8 by choosing the Ground option on your ATC menu.

# 4

# Choosing and Flying Your Aircraft

Explore the myriad aircraft that you can fly in Microsoft Flight Simulator 2020, find out what makes a plane appropriate for a particular pilot, and choose the plane that's right for you.

Discover the information you need to gather while you make plans and choices for your flight path and parameters such as fuel supply and payload.

Find out how to use your radio for communication with air traffic control (ATC) and other air traffic throughout your flight.

Get familiar with general flight rules and flight etiquette (especially when playing with others), and recognize behaviors to avoid if you want to fly safely.

IN THIS CHAPTER

» Choosing from your standard
  plane options

» Mulling over aircraft specs and
  specialties

» Deciding which aircraft is right
  for you

# Chapter **12**

# Airplane! (Not the Movie, the Craft)

Microsoft Flight Simulator 2020 offers one of the most realistic flight experiences you can have without climbing into a cockpit. In addition to exploring any destination across the globe, you get a variety of planes. Whether that means you hop into a commercial airliner or take it slow with a more modest-sized plane, there's something out there for any player.

Maybe you flew in a massive Airbus that was super comfortable, and you want to recreate that situation somehow. Or perhaps you'd rather try flying something a bit smaller. This sim can help make all your flight-related dreams come true — thanks to its healthy selection of aircrafts.

If you're reading this book, you may not even know what planes you can choose from yet. We've got your back. In this chapter, you can explore the plethora of aircrafts that Flight Simulator offers. The coolest part? You don't need millions to fly your own personal plane. How many people can say *that?*

# Pick a Craft, Any Craft

Are you ready to choose an aircraft to kick off your time within the world of Flight Simulator? All you need to do is decide, so consider the information in this chapter, keeping the following questions in mind:

>> Which aircraft are the easiest for beginners?

>> Which planes can fly the highest?

>> Which craft can travel fastest?

>> Which planes demand the least (or most) attention for control?

These are all valid questions that anyone looking to select a plane asks at some point. Make your aircraft choice by weighing the importance (to you) of the answers.

# Planes, Planes, and More Planes

You can find a ton of plane models in the world, and a number of them are represented in Microsoft Flight Simulator. Table 12-1 offers a quick look at the types of aircraft and their primary uses.

**TABLE 12-1**      **Standard Microsoft Flight Simulator Aircraft**

| Aircraft Type | Power and Use |
|---|---|
| Airliners | Created specifically to transport passengers and cargo, airliners have jet engines and go on relatively lengthier flights between major airports and hubs. |
| Jets | Propelled by jet engines, jets are most efficient at speeds close to or above the speed of sound. Different types of jets — turbojets, turbofans, and rockets — are used for different purposes. |
| Turboprops | Also used as transport, turboprops have a turbine engine to drive an aircraft propeller, operate at speeds similar to smaller airliners, and burn one-third less fuel per passenger. |
| Propellers | Three types of propellers — fixed pitch, constant speed, and ground adjustable — use corkscrew-like aerodynamic devices that resemble giant fans. Propeller aircraft are common in general (non-commercial) aviation. |

Choosing which plane to fly first can feel like a massive decision. Like a kid trying to decide which present to open first on Christmas morning, you might freeze from indecision when making an aircraft choice. You just have *so many* choices. To help you decide on an aircraft, the following sections give you specifics on the makes and models that the game includes by default, and a little more information about how they work. Who knows? You just might end up knowing more about them than the flight sim pros in your friend group.

## Airliners

True to their name, airliners are usually operated by major airlines around the world. The largest airliners are actually wide-body jets that are also called *twin-aisle* airliners, which refers to the two separate aisles running from the front to the back of the passenger cabin.

The single-aisle, or narrow body airliner is typically used for short- to medium-distance flights that require less space for passengers overall. These airliners can get even smaller, too — those that belong to regional airlines might seat fewer than 100 passengers and can rely on turbofans or turboprops, like some of the smaller planes found in the game. (See the section "Propellers," later in this chapter, for more on these smaller planes.)

Airliners that may come with Flight Simulator include

>> **Airbus A320neo:** The best-selling jet of all time, topping the Boeing 737.

>> **Boeing 747-8 Intercontinental:** The world's fastest commercial jet, according to Boeing.

>> **Boeing 787-10 Dreamliner:** Contains the largest windows of all available commercial jets.

TECHNICAL
STUFF

The major airliner manufacturers around the globe include Airbus (UK/France/Germany/Spain), Boeing (United States), Bombardier Aerospace (Canada), Embraer (Brazil), and Mitsubishi Aircraft Corporation (Japan). The Boeing 247 was crafted as the first modern airline, with all-metal construction and fully retractable landing gear, while the Boeing 207 was the first with a pressurized cabin.

## Jets

What's the difference between a regular airplane and a jet? All jets are planes, but not all planes are jets. Although most modern planes have jet engines, not every airliner is classified as a jet. When compared with propeller-powered aircraft, jets fly at higher speeds, have slower response times with more lift, and have a considerably shorter takeoff.

Table 12-1 notes three main types of jets — turbojets, turbofans, and rockets — but the jets you encounter in Flight Simulator are more akin to airliner-esque planes you normally see soaring through the air. Both from Textron Aviation, two jets that Flight Simulator offers are

>> **Cessna Citation Longitude:** A business-class jet that's a favorite of celebrities and corporate entities.

>> **Cessna Citation CJ4:** Features the highest range out of the entire Cessna CJ jet family.

You can find plenty of business-class jets in Flight Simulator, but you can also download and try out the F/A-18 Super Hornet as featured in the film *Top Gun: Maverick* (2022) — if you feel the need for speed.

The turbojet-powered Heinkel He 178 — first flown on August 27, 1939 — was the world's first jet aircraft. The world now has a variety of different types of jet aircrafts, for both civilians and members of the military.

## Turboprops

A turboprop plane uses a turbine engine to drive an aircraft propeller, and it usually operates at speeds below 450 miles per hour (mph). These planes have a pretty complicated assembly. Turboprop engines need to include an intake, combustor, turbine, reduction gearbox, and a propelling nozzle to work properly. Figure 12-1 shows a turboprop aircraft from the game.

When air is drawn into the engine intake, it's then compressed. Fuel is added to the combustor, which is added to the compressed air already inside. This leads to combustion, which creates hot combustion gases that are sent out through the rear of the engine.

Turboprop airplanes that come standard with Flight Simulator include

>> **Daher TBM 930:** Considered the fastest single-engine production airplane in existence when it debuted in 2016.

FIGURE 12-1:
A turboprop
plane in flight
in Microsoft
Flight
Simulator.

>> **Beechcraft King Air 350i:** Known as one of the most fuel-efficient aircrafts for business users, with the ability to land on shorter runways than jets.

>> **208 B Grand Caravan EX:** Originally engineered for shorter, rough runways and to be used during more challenging missions.

## Propellers

You've likely heard the term *propeller* before, or you might have something in your home or garden that looks like it: a giant fan. Propeller planes use these giant, fan-like devices to convert energy into a force that creates thrust.

All planes you fly that use this type of energy and mechanism operate much in the same manner. You need to be mindful of how best to control any propeller-driven craft that you're flying, of course, but with some practice, it becomes second nature.

Many propeller planes come standard with Flight Simulator and represent a slew of manufacturers. Table 12-2 offers a (hopefully) straightforward view of aircraft choices (in various Flight Simulator editions) in this category.

**TABLE 12-2**    **Propeller Aircraft in Flight Simulator**

| From this Manufacturer | This Model | Use in the Real World |
|---|---|---|
| Aviat | Pitts Special S2S | Aerobatics |
| Cirrus | SR22 | General aviation |
| Cub | Crafter X Cub | General aviation |
| Diamond Aircraft | DA40-TDI | General aviation |
| | DA40NG | General aviation |
| | DA62 | General aviation |
| | DV20 | General aviation |
| Extra | 330LT | Aerobatics |
| Flight Design | CTSL | Ultralight |
| ICON | A5 | Ultralight |
| JBM Aircraft | VL-3 | Ultralight |
| Junkers | Ju 52 | Hauling |
| Pipistrel | Virus SW 121 | General aviation |
| Robin | Cap10 | Aerobatics |
| | DR400/100 Cadet | General aviation |
| Textron Aviation | Beechcraft Bonanza G36 | General aviation |
| | Beechcraft Baron G58: | General aviation |
| | Cessna 152 | General aviation |
| | Cessna 152 Aerobat | Aerobatics |
| | Cessna 172 Skyhawk | General aviation |
| | Cessna 172 Skyhawk (G1000) | General aviation |
| Zlin Aviation | Savage Cub | General aviation |
| | Shock Ultra | Ultralight |

# Different Planes for Different Pilots

You're ready to fly the friendly skies. You've overcome your fear and are ready to jump in, get both feet wet, and (hopefully) not drown in a ton of new plane-related information. Your first order of business: Choose a plane to fly. Choosing a plane may sound simple but can be deceptively hard, especially if you don't know a lot about aircraft.

REMEMBER

No one has a one-size-fits-all option when it comes to choosing a plane that you want to fly. But you don't have to worry about making a right or wrong selection. If the plane doesn't fit what you're looking for, you can choose another! It doesn't matter if you choose a plane that you may never learn to fly in the real world, as long as you (and any gaming partner) have fun.

My goal is to make choosing a Flight Simulator aircraft as easy as possible. These following sections offer a few streamlined picks (with added superlatives) based on aircraft capabilities and benefits for pilots. But don't worry — you can try them all, eventually. After you get a taste for flying, you won't be able to stop!

## Best for Beginners: Cessna 152

Flight Simulator serves up the Textron Aviation Cessna 152 plane, shown in Figure 12-2, as the one you use to complete the game's initial tutorials for a reason. Learning to fly by using this plane is a lot simpler than learning on many other planes on the list, especially for complete beginners. Not only does the Cessna 152 feature excellent handling, but also its cruise speed of 107 knots true airspeed (KTAS) and max altitude of 14,700 ft make it a versatile option for just about any shorter flight.

If you need practice landing on the runway efficiently, the Cessna 152 is an awesome pick. It works well with smaller runways, and it offers stability even when you're not completely in control. So whether you want to use autopilot or try your hand at righting the ship, so to speak, the Cessna 152 makes it one smooth ride.

FIGURE 12-2:
The Textron Aviation Cessna 152 plane, great for beginning players.

## Best for high altitudes: Cessna Citation Longitude

If you want to go as high as you possibly can in the sky, you have only one real option: the Cessna Citation Longitude. This light business jet is a favorite because it can rise so ridiculously high in the sky (45,000 feet, to be exact). It's the only plane in the game that can reach those heights.

The Cessna Citation Longitude also happens to be quite capable of some impressive speeds, with a cruising speed of 895 KTAS and a top speed of 1,037 KTAS. On top of that, you can figure out how to fly it relatively easily, unlike some of its more complex counterparts. Go high and go fast with the Cessna Citation Longitude.

## Best for performing tricks: Aviat Pitts Special S2S

You can always become an even more fantastic pilot than you already are (even if you're already an expert). Whatever your piloting skill level, if you play Flight Simulator as much as possible, get all your practice in, and experiment a bit here and there, you can soon figure out how to perform more complicated maneuvers.

So if you're no longer a beginner, you may want to show others how great you are at those aileron rolls or loop-de-loops in the air (mind those passengers, please!). Hop into the cockpit of this bad boy, and you might feel like people should be paying to watch your antics.

## Best for long-haul flights: Boeing 787-10 Dreamliner

If you plan to spend quite a bit of time in the sky, look for the most luxurious aircraft possible to serve that purpose: the Boeing 787-10 Dreamliner. This performance-focused plane is quick and efficient, but it's also huge. That size doesn't prevent it from absolutely zipping through the sky, though. With a maximum altitude of 41,100 feet and cruise speed of 495 KTAS, you can be speeding through the air in no time.

So if you're looking for a plane that's a delight to fly from one side of the globe to another, or even just a cross-country trip, you can't go wrong with the Dreamliner. It's in the name after all: It's a dream to fly!

## Best for Intermediate Players: Daher TBM 930

If you've been playing Flight Simulator for some time as a beginner and want to move forward to a more challenging plane, the Daher TBM 930 is an excellent choice. It's faster than the premiere beginner's choice, the Cessna 152 (which you can read about in the section "Best for beginners: Cessna 152," earlier in this chapter), and it's heftier as well. Flying the TBM 930 gives you a chance to get to know how a faster and heftier plane feels in the air before moving on to an even bigger plane.

The TBM 930 is great for both short and long-distance trips, and it's attractive, to boot. You can appreciate its 330 KTAS cruising speed and maximum altitude of 31,000 feet, while avoiding the feeling that you've bitten off more than you can chew for your first few next-level outings.

## Best all-purpose plane: Beechcraft Baron G58

If you want to fly a plane that ticks all the boxes but doesn't excel too much in one area over another, the Beechcraft Baron G58, shown in Figure 12-3, is the cockpit you want to jump into. It zips at a 176 KTAS cruising speed, and it maxes out at 20,688-foot altitude. Despite its zip, you can navigate with the G58 pretty simply. It isn't too hefty, has good range, and after a little practice, you can handle the plane in the air quite well.

**FIGURE 12-3:** The Beechcraft Baron G58; a fabulous all-purpose plane.

# Best turboprop: Cessna 208 B Grand Caravan EX

Turboprops can make for some very interesting flights. They're great for anyone who's been spending more time in the cockpit than most, and they offer some truly unique handling. The Cessna 208 B Grand Caravan EX is much larger than a standard propeller plane, although its size doesn't make a difference when it's in the air.

The single-engine design may seem like it doesn't have the juice to keep you moving forward, but on the contrary, the Cessna 208 Caravan has more than enough power for you to get from point A to point B. And you don't need an entire hour of fiddling around in its cockpit to become comfortable with operating this plane.

# Best for showing off: ICON A5

Some planes are decidedly flashier than others. If you're into the aesthetics of planes, then you need to try out the debonair ICON A5, shown in Figure 12-4. This aircraft looks less like a typical propeller plane and more like one that's pumped and primed for racing. If you're into the sleek look, you should appreciate that aspect.

The ICON A5 is a little on the smaller side — which makes it great for beginners — and has limited speed, along with a smaller fuel tank. But if you decide to climb into it, you can look forward to some zippy, show-off rides while you practice some finer maneuvers in the air. Your friends will be so proud of you.

**FIGURE 12-4:** The ICON A5 plane is one of the flashier designs you can choose.

Chapter **13**

# Knowing the Nitty-Gritty of Flight Planning and Navigation

B efore you can set off flying in Microsoft Flight Simulator 2020, you need to lay the groundwork for your flight. Preparations include not only planning your flight path, but also completing any briefings from air traffic control (ATC) and taking in other informational notices from providers such as the Automatic Terminal Information Service (ATIS). All this data can help you understand what flight routes and conditions you may encounter.

Depending on the type of flight you're planning or wanting to complete, how much information you need can change drastically. For example, if you want to fly across the U.S. in a twin engine prop plane, you definitely need to find out about appropriate waypoint airports that have fuel available for your refueling needs. Nevertheless, having a good eye for what details to seek out helps you lay the foundation for your flight and get the process moving and the plane up in the air as quickly as possible.

In this chapter, I show you how to obtain the information you need, including the briefing for your flight, as well as other important travel planning specifics. For example, you need to know your travel altitude, how to direct your flight path, how to deal with inclement weather when it pops up, and how to actually navigate your flight plan.

# Gathering Information for the Flight You Want to Take

Keeping on top of all the information that affects your flight is vital to its success. If you want to pull off a correctly executed flight, you need to keep a constant check-in with air traffic control (ATC) and an awareness of the weather, altitude, fuel, and overall weight your craft contains. All of this data can change how your plane flies, and thus how long it can stay in the air by using that single tank of fuel, though many planes have auxiliary fuel tanks to combat this issue. Figure 13-1 shows the ATC window from an aircraft cockpit.

**FIGURE 13-1:**
Keeping in constant contact with ATC ensures up-to-date information.

**REMEMBER**

If you want to become a successful and skilled pilot, you must know how to keep track of all of the information that affects flight planning and execution of that plan.

# Choosing your flight rules: IFR versus VFR

If you're flying based on Instrument Flight Rules (IFR), then you need to follow whatever orders and commands come from the air traffic control (ATC) personnel. If you're flying visually, using Visual Flight Rules (VFR), then you're responsible for paying attention to the wind, rain, and general weather around you, as well as other air traffic and your physical surroundings. Check the conditions around the airport — visually and through weather reporting services — before attempting to take off, and always be mindful of the changing environment during your flight.

With instrument-based flight, you continue to follow ATC commands throughout the entirety of your flight. And so, ATC advises you of any incoming weather conditions or air traffic issues that you need to worry about before takeoff and during the flight. See Figure 13-2 for a look at the ATC window when preparing for takeoff.

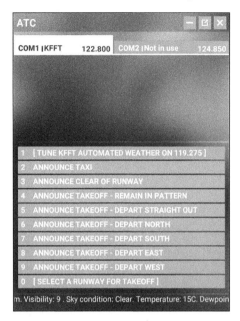

**FIGURE 13-2:**
Tuning in the ATC window for local weather conditions.

Pilots usually set up an IFR flight plan to avoid any incoming traffic in the air, which you absolutely need to do to avoid accidents in flight. With IFR, you're much more reliant on the instructions that ATC provides and must adapt communications to contact and get instructions from the appropriate controllers when you change to new regions of airspace. If you follow the instructions that ATC gives you, you shouldn't run into any issues. See Chapter 10 for more information about the role of ATC at the airport. Figure 13-3 shows the communications with the ATC control tower at Louisville during a landing sequence.

If you want to successfully fly by using VFR, you need to know how to tell where you are based on the environment and landmarks around you. Private aircraft commonly use VFR, and if you want to really take control of where you're heading, it's a great choice because you don't have to file a detailed flight plan. However, flying with VFR can also be exceptionally dangerous. You navigate based on the landmarks and world around you — with a bit of help from your instruments and ATC. Figure 13-4 shows a well-known U.S. landmark that you might reference when flying near New York City.

Steer clear of clouds and keep an eye out for landmarks that you recognize to help you navigate to the correct airport. And, if you do end up having some trouble, you can always contact ATC to get some updated instructions. But, if you really want to rely on your visual skills and navigational instincts, VFR flying is one of the best ways to do so.

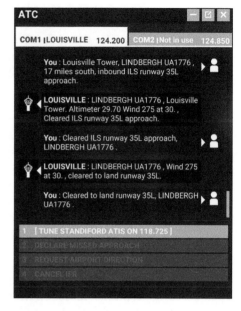

FIGURE 13-3:
ATC landing instructions.

## Departure airports, waypoints, and arrival airports

When planning your flight you can choose from a number of locations, including your departure airport, waypoints, arrival airport, and even which airport runway you want to start off from (if an airport has multiple runways to choose from). Figure 13-5 shows that the Bombardier CRJ550ER plans to depart KJFK airport in New York via runway 22R.

FIGURE 13-4:
Navigating by landmarks is vital to flying based on visual rules.

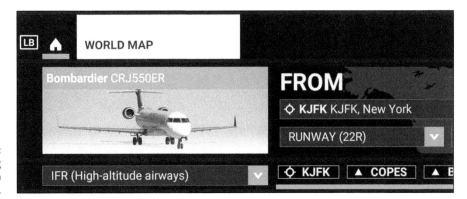

When planning flight paths, keep an eye out for stops that just don't make sense along your current route:

>> **Stops that require you to travel back in the opposite direction you were headed.** Backtracking only causes additional delays in reaching your final destination.

>> **Stops that can't accommodate your aircraft.** Plan ahead based on the type of aircraft you're flying because not every aircraft can land at every runway or airport. Make sure that the airports at which you're planning to make layovers and stops can accommodate the size of the aircraft that you're planning to fly.

See Chapter 8 for ideas on choosing and familiarizing yourself with airports. Figure 13-6 depicts an efficient and effective flight path from KJFK (JFK International Airport in New York) to KLAX (Los Angeles International in California).

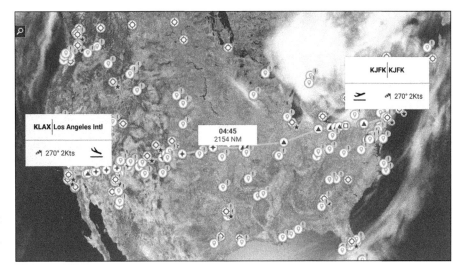

# Getting an altitude

Your travel altitude, or *cruising altitude*, is the altitude at which you spend the majority of your flight. This altitude can vary based on a number of things, including but not limited to

>> **The type of aircraft you're flying:** All aircraft have limits on how high they can fly. Smaller airplanes such as a Cessna 172 may have a service ceiling around 14,000 feet. A larger commercial plane such as a Boeing 787 may fly as high as 43,000 feet.

>> **The flight path that you plan:** When your flight path takes you westbound (between 180 and 360 degrees), ATC assigns altitudes by even thousands of feet, such as 20,000 feet. When your heading is eastbound (between 0 and 180 degrees), your assigned altitude is an odd number of thousands (for example, 25,000 feet).

>> **What kind of weather conditions you're flying into:** For example, ATC advises an altitude based on the presence of cloud layers that affect your flight path if you're flying VFR.

Figure 13-7 shows the altitude assigned at a waypoint along a flight path.

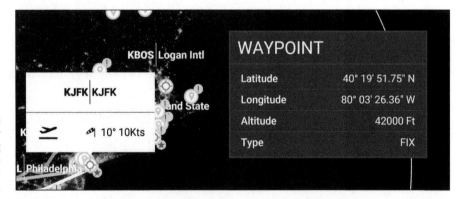

**FIGURE 13-7:** Your cruising altitude changes with every flight.

Either ATC gives you your travel altitude, or you set it up yourself in your flight plan. But just because you have a cruising altitude for your flight plan doesn't mean that you can just take off and immediately make your way to that altitude. You still need to clear your rate of ascent with ATC. Normally, ATC clears you in steps to reach your cruising altitude.

TIP

If you're not sure what travel altitude ATC has cleared you for in your flight plan, you can always check the navigational panel in your aircraft. It always displays the cruising altitude to which ATC has adjusted you. Refer to Figure 13-7 for the navigational panel with altitude display.

## Estimating flight duration

The *estimated flight time* is the amount of time that you can expect your flight to take. *Remember:* Flights that cover a greater distance take more time to complete.

For example, a flight of 900 miles should take around five hours in a Cessna 172 at its max speed of 188 miles per hour. However, it only has a range of around 700 miles, which means you'll need to refuel. If you begin adding stops to that flight, then what looks like a five-hour trip at first glance might take six-to-seven hours or more. Figure 13-8 shows the distance (in nautical miles, NM) and time required to reach various waypoints along a flight path.

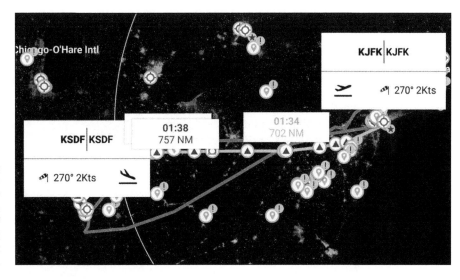

**FIGURE 13-8:** The estimated time can vary depending on the amount of stops you add to your flight plan.

**REMEMBER**

Estimated times can also change if you run into inclement weather or encounter other issues (such as mechanical failures) during flight. You may end up with a flight that takes much longer to complete than you anticipated. And because these virtual flights take real-world time to complete, you need to set aside the play time. In the example flight — 900 miles in a Cessna 172 — it would take almost seven hours to complete the journey.

Here are other factors that affect estimated flight time:

>> **The estimated flight time doesn't include time spent waiting.** For example, the time estimate calculated by the game doesn't include the amount of time you may need to wait (if you're taking off from a busy departure airport) or the amount of time you may need to wait to land at your arrival airport.

>> **You can adjust the Flight Simulator simulation rate to shorten the required flight time.** If you do end up needing to cut your flight a little short, you can always speed up the in-game time by pressing R-Ctrl-plus sign (+) on your keyboard's numpad. This key combination increases the simulation rate. Alternatively, pressing R-Ctrl-minus sign (–) slows down the rate of the simulation.

TIP

If you need to see your estimated flight time or your arrival time while in the midst of a flight, you can press the N key to bring up the Navlog window, which displays several pieces of vital information, including these time estimates. Figure 13-9 shows how a Navlog window appears. (I talk a bit more about the Navlog in the section "Minding your tracking tools," later in this chapter.)

## Noting weather conditions

Weather is a key environmental factor that you encounter when flying in Flight Simulator. Weather can be a boon to your flight (perhaps you get a tailwind that speeds you along) or an obstacle (such as a pop-up storm that blocks your path). Also, storms can slow down takeoff and landing, as well as impede other important parts of navigating an aircraft around the world.

Here are two main aspects of weather to consider while you construct a flight plan:

>> **Weather changes can strike at any moment during a flight.** Your flight may start with clear skies but end up running into a thunderstorm, for example.

Estimated time elapsed

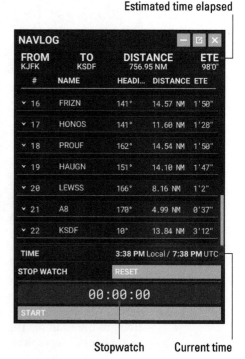

Stopwatch          Current time

**FIGURE 13-9:**
Check your estimated time of arrival in the Navlog at any time.

Always stay up to date on weather information visually — by keeping an eye on weather indicators such as clouds near your flight path — and virtually by checking in with ATC as often as possible.

When you're out flying, keep your eyes and mind open, and always be aware of the color and intensity of clouds around you. After all, you're flying in a massive metal aircraft. Flying into the heart of a thunderstorm, where lightning is flashing across the sky several times a minute, probably isn't going to be a great experience for you or the heavy aircraft that you're trying to pilot. Get clearance from ATC when you're trying to increase or decrease altitude to skirt these kinds of situations.

>> **Weather conditions can greatly affect your flight timing and performance.** Conditions such as wind gusts can blow your aircraft to and fro and create turbulence. Consequently, you may fight with the controls or may need to increase the amount of thrust your aircraft must exert to push through the air, causing you to use more fuel.

Flight Simulator enables you to select custom weather settings. When you do, you choose specific options about the weather, including the altitude where the clouds are, the depth of snow, the percentage of lightning, and the temperature at ground level. Make sure to look into all the options before completing your flight plan. See Figure 13-10 for a look at the Weather window, where you can make custom settings. The section "Setting your flight path and other parameters," later in the chapter, goes into how to find the Weather window and make your choices.

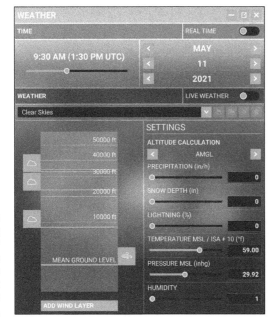

**FIGURE 13-10:** Customizing weather conditions affects the flight challenges you face as a pilot.

# Allowing for passengers and cargo

Passengers and cargo might sound like flight aspects that you can ignore in Flight Simulator, but both actually play a pivotal role in how you plan your flights. When setting your aircraft up for a flight, you not only select your aircraft (see Chapter 12), its livery, and any failures you want to deal with (see Chapter 16), but you also customize your craft's weight and balance.

When you select the Weight and Balance screen from the Aircraft Selection window (see Figure 13-11), you see a broad overview of what to expect from your aircraft's cargo and passenger capabilities. On this screen, you can see the center of gravity (CG) and the positioning and percentages for CG forward and aft limits. These limits help you determine how to distribute your aircraft's load (fuel, cargo, and passengers) while you prepare the airplane to fly properly.

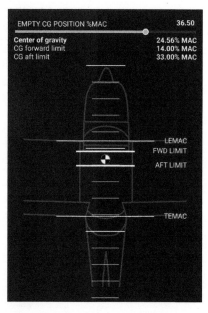

**WARNING**

Having an off-centered center of gravity can cause very unfortunate problems throughout a flight. Redistribute your cargo and passenger load as needed to achieve proper centering. And check the weight totals to ensure that you're not going beyond the max allowable fuel, max payload, or the max takeoff weight, as shown in Figure 13-12, which you can access in the Flight Options menu at the World Map screen.

**FIGURE 13-11:**
The Weight and Balance screen helps you manage your passengers and cargo.

Here are the various weights that you must manage for your flight:

>> **Max Allowable Fuel:** The amount of fuel that your aircraft can hold. You most likely don't need to travel with the max allowable level of fuel in place, depending on the length of your flight. You may choose to carry less fuel because you need that weight for other things, such as passengers and cargo.

**WARNING**

Don't cut your fuel levels too deeply because you may need more fuel than anticipated if you run into inclement weather or for some other reason need to stay in the air longer.

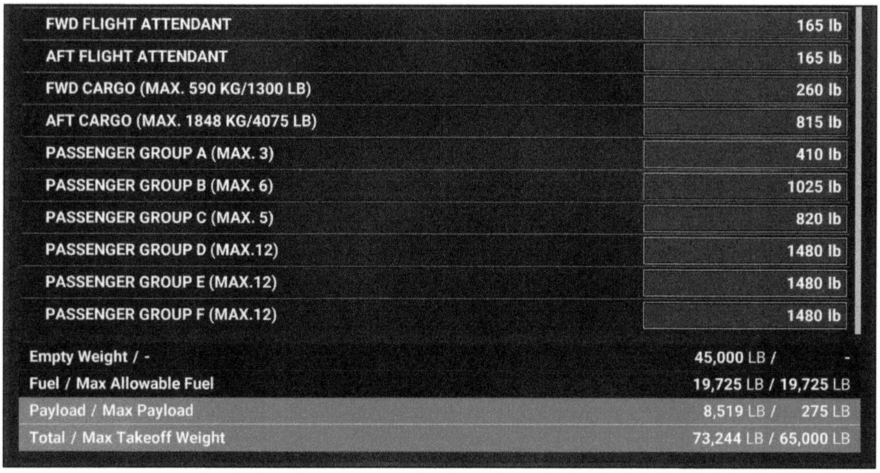

| | |
|---|---|
| FWD FLIGHT ATTENDANT | 165 lb |
| AFT FLIGHT ATTENDANT | 165 lb |
| FWD CARGO (MAX. 590 KG/1300 LB) | 260 lb |
| AFT CARGO (MAX. 1848 KG/4075 LB) | 815 lb |
| PASSENGER GROUP A (MAX. 3) | 410 lb |
| PASSENGER GROUP B (MAX. 6) | 1025 lb |
| PASSENGER GROUP C (MAX. 5) | 820 lb |
| PASSENGER GROUP D (MAX.12) | 1480 lb |
| PASSENGER GROUP E (MAX.12) | 1480 lb |
| PASSENGER GROUP F (MAX.12) | 1480 lb |
| Empty Weight / - | 45,000 LB / - |
| Fuel / Max Allowable Fuel | 19,725 LB / 19,725 LB |
| Payload / Max Payload | 8,519 LB / 275 LB |
| Total / Max Takeoff Weight | 73,244 LB / 65,000 LB |

**FIGURE 13-12:** Keep an eye on the maximum weights of your aircraft while you make changes.

>> **Max Payload:** The maximum amount of weight that you can have in cargo. This weight includes not only your passengers, but also the baggage cargo that they have.

>> **Maximum Takeoff Weight:** The heaviest your aircraft can be before it just can't take off. You don't necessarily want to reach this maximum weight (lighter is better because less lift is required to take off), so try to adjust the level of fuel that you really need, as well as the level of payload that you're running with.

Each and every aircraft has a different Max Payload and Max Allowable Fuel weight, and these two weights, along with the base weight of the aircraft, help determine the Maximum Takeoff Weight.

# Planning and Navigating Your Flight by the Important Details

The devil is in the details — you've probably heard that saying at one point or another in your life, and it's absolutely true for flight planning in Flight Simulator. Plan out your flight path and parameters and be aware of all the expectations (for example, knowing which way to turn after taking off) that you're responsible for before you set out on your flight. You can read about these details of flight planning in the following section.

REMEMBER As the pilot in command, plan ahead by gathering information for airport and weather conditions, amount of fuel needed, accommodations for cargo or passengers, and headings to follow for the course you plan to take (see the section "Gathering Information for the Flight You Want to Take," earlier in this chapter). Figure 13-13 shows various flight paths leaving from JFK International Airport in New York.

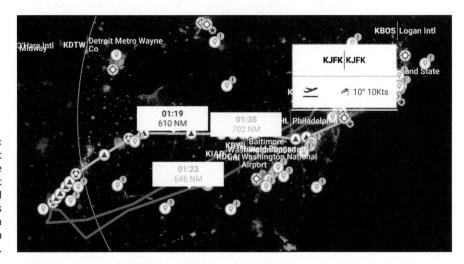

**FIGURE 13-13:** Your flight path is one of the most important and basic pieces of information you need as a pilot.

## Setting your flight path and other parameters

Planning your flight path is one of the most important aspects of being a pilot in Flight Simulator. Not only do you determine where you're starting from and where you're going, but you also decide what stops to make along the way.

For example, you can choose airports to use for layovers and special places that you want to visit along your route. This last part is especially true if you're taking a sightseeing flight. Alternatively, you can auto-generate a VFR or IFR flight plan by choosing from the drop-down menu under the current aircraft section in the World Map.

Assuming that you already chose an aircraft to fly (I talk about picking an aircraft in Chapter 12), decided on the flight rules (VFR or IFR) to follow (discussed in Chapter 11), and gathered information regarding flight conditions (see Chapter 8) for your flight path, your game parameters, and other aspects of your flight:

1. **From the World Map (which you access from the Main Menu), set the endpoints and waypoints for your flight by clicking on the World Map and making the appropriate selections.**

2. **Select the Flight Conditions box near the top-right of the World Map menu.**

3. **In the menu that appears, set up big-picture parameters for companion players (or not) and other air traffic (or not) during your virtual flight.**

   Select the appropriate Multiplayer option (the buttons on the left in Figure 13-14) if you want to fly the friendly (virtual) skies with others (see Chapter 5 for a look at taking multiplayer flights):

   Choose from these Air Traffic options (the buttons on the right in Figure 13-14):

   - *Live Traffic:* Air Traffic data is based on real-world data and communications.

   - *AI:* Lets the game decide Air Traffic data and generate it randomly.

   - *Off:* When you select this option, you don't have to worry about Air Traffic data at all.

**FIGURE 13-14:**
Selections for the players and air traffic you want to experience on your flight.

4. **From the same Flight Conditions pop-up window, choose from the Weather and Time parameters for your flight.**

   At the bottom-left of the window, you can find these options (see Figure 13-15):

   - *Live:* Weather for the areas that you travel through is based on real-world meteorological data. Select this option if you want to experience the simulated world as truly and close to reality as possible.

   - *Preset:* Choose from a list of preset options for cloud cover, precipitation, and so on. These options include Live Weather, Clear Skies, Few Clouds, Scattered Clouds, Broken Clouds, High Level Clouds, Overcast, Rain, Snow, and Storm.

   - *Custom:* For custom weather settings, you set up the type of weather you want by using the sliders to set conditions (which can vary per altitude).

5. **In the Weather window (flip back to Figure 13-10), customize your Time and Weather settings.**

This menu provides you with all the weather option information and has the defaults Real Time and Live Weather selected. You can always customize settings:

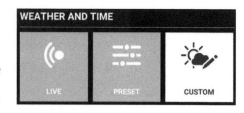

FIGURE 13-15:
For a more controlled flight, set up the weather that you want to encounter.

- Switch off the Real Time toggle, and then set your own date and time by adjusting the settings.

- Switch off Live Weather to choose your own conditions from the settings provided.

6. **Open the Aircraft selection menu and click in the left column to open the Weights and Balance window.**

7. **Make selections for the amount of fuel to carry and distribution of passengers and cargo to optimize your weight and balance. (Refer back to Figure 13-12.)**

The more fuel you carry, the farther you can go, but your plane will also be heavier. The more your plane weighs, the more sluggish it flies, which is why pilots often choose to fly with just enough fuel to reach their destination and loiter for a bit.

REMEMBER

Before takeoff, make sure that your flight planning takes fuel levels into account. You may need more fuel than you start with to reach your final destination; this happens often on longer flights and means that you have to set down at an airport midway just to refuel.

8. **To prepare for your flight, use your radio channels by bringing up the ATC window to communicate with the tower.**

REMEMBER

The information presented in your preflight briefing can change, especially when it comes to weather conditions. Keep a watchful eye on the sky and listen out for any changes from ATC.

9. **Listen to the region's ATIS information by tuning to the channel in the ATC/Radio window.**

Pay attention to the current wind and weather, active runways and their conditions, potential delays, and so on for departing and arriving air traffic.

When you're ready to fly, see Chapter 11 for a rundown of the takeoff process.

# Navigating your flight with help from Flight Simulator

To navigate successfully in Flight Simulator, you need to do more than just plan the perfect flight path, choose game parameters, and manage your aircraft's weight (all discussed in the preceding section). There's a lot that goes into properly navigating your way across the world from airport to airport. When flying Instrument Flight Rules (IFR), your instruments and communications, and your Navlog window, give you the key to success. For Visual Flight Rules (VFR) flying, recognizing the world around you and keeping an eye on landmarks and surrounding weather is most important.

## Making the most of your console instruments

When navigating in Flight Simulator, the console in your aircraft (see Figure 13-16) has all the information you need to keep up with your fuel levels, your heading, and (of course) your current cruising altitude (which I discuss in section "Getting an altitude," earlier in this chapter).

Engine status            Radar

**FIGURE 13-16:** Your console instruments — from the compass to the altimeter — provide important navigation information.

**REMEMBER** Become familiar with your console instruments so that you can easily monitor essential flight components — such as the direction you're heading, how high you are, and even how fast you're going — which help you adhere to your carefully planned course.

## Minding your tracking tools

Your fuel gauge is an important dial that keeps track of how much fuel is available for your aircraft. Especially if you're taking part in longer flights, you may need to refuel along the way. Watch the fuel gauge. If you didn't set up a designated airport for refueling but the gauge shows that your supply is getting low (see Figure 13-17), you may need to find a nearby airport where you can land and refill your tank.

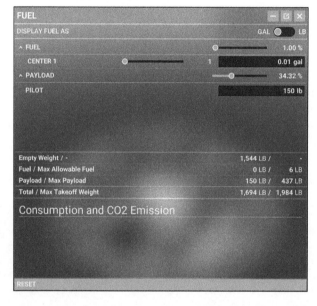

**FIGURE 13-17:**
Use your fuel gauge as a point of reference to ensure that you're never running low.

**REMEMBER**

Conserving fuel and using it as efficiently as possible are important actions you take as the pilot in command of your aircraft. Although what preset you select for weather conditions might not seem that important to navigation, any ongoing adverse weather conditions that you're dealing with can drastically affect your fuel usage and, therefore, your navigation prowess. Running out of fuel in the middle of a flight is never fun — for you, your passengers, or your airplane.

**TIP**

You can change how much fuel your aircraft carries at takeoff from the Flight Planning window, which you access when you select the aircraft that you want to fly. See Chapter 12 for the rundown on choosing and plane (and fuel capacity).

You may be tempted to ignore a tool like your Navlog, shown in Figure 13-18, because it requires a lot of attention when you'd probably rather be staring out the window. But using it can provide vital information while in-flight. Access your Navlog window by pressing the icon that looks like a clock in the top toolbar in-game and check it often to keep up with your updated estimated arrival time, current location, distance between waypoints, and other key pieces of information that you may need while navigating your trip.

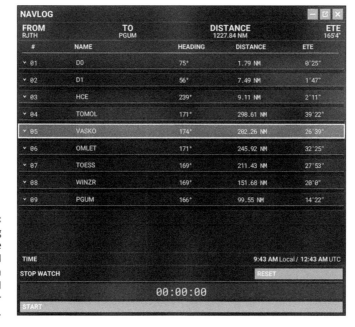

| FROM | | TO | | DISTANCE | | ETE |
| RJTH | | PGUM | | 1227.84 NM | | 165'4" |
| # | NAME | | HEADING | DISTANCE | ETE | |
| ⌄ 01 | D0 | | 75° | 1.79 NM | 0'25" | |
| ⌄ 02 | D1 | | 56° | 7.49 NM | 1'47" | |
| ⌄ 03 | HCE | | 239° | 9.11 NM | 2'11" | |
| ⌄ 04 | TOMOL | | 171° | 298.61 NM | 39'22" | |
| ⌄ 05 | VASKO | | 174° | 282.26 NM | 26'39" | |
| ⌄ 06 | OMLET | | 171° | 245.92 NM | 32'25" | |
| ⌄ 07 | TOESS | | 169° | 211.43 NM | 27'53" | |
| ⌄ 08 | WINZR | | 169° | 151.68 NM | 20'0" | |
| ⌄ 09 | PGUM | | 166° | 99.55 NM | 14'22" | |

TIME — 9:43 AM Local / 12:43 AM UTC

STOP WATCH — RESET

00:00:00

START

FIGURE 13-18: The Navlog is one of the most useful but often overlooked tools at your disposal.

Chapter **14**

# Working the Radio in Single or Multiplayer Mode

peaking with air traffic control (ATC) personnel is an important skill to acquire in Microsoft Flight Simulator 2020. Not only does this vital radio contact allow you to get off (and back on) the ground safely, but it also guides your flight while you check in with the operator throughout your trip. Figuring out the ins and outs of radio communication with ATC is essential for every budding pilot. Check out Chapter 11 for information specific to talking with ATC during takeoff and landing.

In this chapter, I introduce the basics of talking via the radio in Flight Simulator while your flight progresses, and I also discuss some general tips and tricks about radio chatter when flying in multiplayer mode. For example, you need to be aware that other players' communications with ATC may intermingle with your own; being patient and waiting your turn are good habits for a careful and considerate pilot.

# Calling Up the Radio

You can communicate with ATC or the regional operators while in flight at any time by bringing up the Radio menu (also known as the ATC/Radio menu). Depending on the configuration of your playing platform, you may be able to call up the radio panel by simply pressing the Scroll Lock button on your keyboard; this *keybind* (meaning a key or keys tied to specific game actions, as discussed in Chapter 2) is the default setting when you're using a keyboard). You can also input all the stations manually by using your airplane's simulated radios, like those shown in Figure 14-1. Alternatively, you may need to bring up the radio panel through the top menu bar.

REMEMBER

You can realistically change your radio channels in Flight Simulator by interacting with the radio console in your plane's cockpit. However, doing so is much less convenient than using the ATC/Radio menu to autotune stations.

**FIGURE 14-1:**
The radio panel in an aircraft.

While in flight, you can pull up your Radio menu any time to check in with the various regions of airspace that you're flying through. Here, you can contact operators for assistance and directions. ATC will typically only contact you for altitude clearance changes and handoffs. Such messages are referred to as *callouts*. If you need to discuss flight following or any other additional information that may affect your flight, you need to contact ATC yourself.

# Knowing what to listen for

When you're out flying along your designated flight path, keep an ear (or eye) open for any callouts issued by the regional radio operators of the areas you're flying through (see Figure 14-2). These messages can relay critical data — such as changes to your flight plan — that you must know, for example, to make a necessary change in altitude or heading.

Here are some common ATC callouts you may experience while following your flight plan:

>> Taxi instructions

>> Takeoff clearance

>> Altitude changes and restrictions

**FIGURE 14-2:**
You can easily miss ATC callouts, but the ATC window helps.

## Listening for other aircraft

When you're flying in multiplayer mode, you need to listen out for ATC callouts not only for your aircraft, but also for other planes in your area, to avoid any traffic issues when landing. Additionally, be aware that there may be a delay in response from ATC if you try to reach out to the tower when others are doing the same. Just like in real life, the ATC can only respond to so many people at the same time.

When you find yourself running into interference from other air traffic, you must wait your turn. For example, in many large airports that serve as cargo hubs, you may have to wait 10 to 15 minutes at a time while ATC coordinates the takeoff and landing of multiple planes.

TECHNICAL
STUFF

Some mods available for Flight Simulator allow players to take over as the ATC operator. When they do, things can get more serious because the player/ATC operator may be expecting you to use and understand radio traffic as if you were a real pilot. I want you to be aware of the potential that mods provide, but for the sake of brevity, I don't go in depth on mods in this chapter.

# How to Communicate by Using Your Radio

After you open the ATC/Radio menu (by using the top bar or the appropriate keybind), you can select from a list of commands and radio chatter (shown in Figure 14-3) that you see. For the most part, these commands are similar to menu commands that you may be acquainted with from the other flight-related activities in this book. Each command elicits a response from the ATC operator; listen and pay attention to this response because failing to do so might result in ATC ceasing to provide you with flight services.

For example, if you choose the Pushback command, the in-game ATC operator responds by sending a tractor to push your plane back from the gate or stand where it's parked.

FIGURE 14-3:
Keep in contact with ATC and regional operators while out on your flight.

TIP

The radio is your lifeline when you're landing, taking off, and flying. Keep the ATC/Radio menu handy by resizing it to fit your screen without obstructing (too much) of your vision so that you don't miss out on important communication that's happening on the radio.

# Flying the Friendly Skies with Company

One aspect where Flight Simulator excels is multiplayer mode (previous install-ments didn't do it as well). At any point before a flight, you can choose to fly through the world with other players. This ability adds an additional bit of realism to the flight (notice the other players' aircraft called out in Figure 14-4) because you need to channel your radio comms around others in the area.

Player name, aircraft type, and location

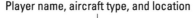
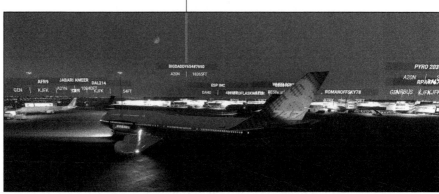

FIGURE 14-4: Multiplayer mode opens a whole new world of immersion in Flight Simulator.

**REMEMBER**

You may find flying while surrounded by other players in multiplayer mode espe-cially tricky when you're landing or taking off, but having this experience gives that real-world feel that many players want to get from flight sims.

If you're planning on playing multiplayer Flight Simulator, keep these tips in mind:

>> **Be respectful of other pilots sharing your airspace.** Most everyone is here to enjoy themselves and make the most of the systems that the game has to offer. Don't cut off others when they're communicating and stay patient when waiting for responses from ATC and regional radio operations.

>> **Watch out for grief coming from other players.** You won't always experi-ence intra-game conflicts; however, keep an eye out for players who may want to *troll* (cause another player grief) or cause issues with your flight.

For example, another player might try to fly on top of you and obstruct your vision. Try to avoid such players when possible; they could easily crash your plane or veer you off course in some other way.

>> **Wait patiently for your turn to take off or land.** Airports have a limited number of runways, which means you may need to take turns landing or taking off when other pilots in multiplayer mode are coming and going from that airport. Waiting for a clear runway can take a while, especially if you've chosen a popular airport. Figure 14-5 shows a series of planes in line for takeoff.

Airplane 2    Airplane 3    Airplane 4    Airplane 1 (on runway)

**FIGURE 14-5:** Some airports may require you to wait to land or take off.

REMEMBER

Being patient is especially important if you're playing with a mod that allows other players to take over the ATC. Wait your turn when landing or taking off. If you find yourself getting static feedback from the radio when requesting taxi, takeoff, or landing instructions, give it a few moments and try again. Hearing static usually means that ATC is currently talking with someone else, and you need to wait for the air to clear, so to speak.

TIP

ATC autotuning is on by default. With this setting on, you can determine what channel the ATC and regional operators are on much more easily. (Figuring out channels can be a sore spot for newer players who aren't used to navigating the system.)

# Chapter **15**

# Rules, Rules, Rules — So Many Rules!

lying in Microsoft Flight Simulator 2020 isn't exactly the same experience as really flying, but it comes close. One area that differs greatly involves following the rules: Flight Simulator doesn't require you to follow all the myriad rules of traditional aviation. However, that doesn't mean you should avoid knowing about those rules. Abide by them regardless. Even if you're not penalized for ignoring certain procedures, playing as if you follow them can make your virtual flights a more real-world experience. After all, the entire point of a simulation like this is to get as close to real life as possible.

In this chapter, I go over some of the rules followed in traditional aviation, as well as touching on some dangerous practices that you want to avoid doing any time you're flying in Flight Simulator. Keeping these rules in mind not only makes your flights much smoother, but it also helps you avoid any potential issues when playing with other players online or tackling an unfamiliar aircraft or route when taking your Flight Simulator experience to the next level.

# Playing It Safe by Following the Rules

Traditional aviation has a ton of rules to keep in mind. So many, in fact, that this book can't include them all — that would be an entire book of its own. Instead, I introduce some of the most important rules, and then show you how you can translate those to help ensure a safe flying experience in Flight Simulator.

## Rules of traditional aviation

The Code of Federal Regulations (CFR) includes the regulations created and endorsed by the departments and agencies of the U.S. federal government. A section of the CFR, the Federal Aviation Regulations (FARs), contains the rules that the Federal Aviation Administration (FAA) prescribes for governing aviation activities in the U.S.

The CFR is always evolving, which means that the rules and regulations for aviation are always changing, too. But despite the changes, you still need to become aware of the basic rules that don't change.

The basic rules involve being mindful of how you behave and train for flying, and how you operate the aircraft that you're responsible for. In general, these rules mainly involve common sense and safety protocols:

>> **No one can operate an aircraft in a careless or reckless manner that endangers another person's life or property.** Just because you think turning at a steep angle would be cool or you want to attempt to take part in stunts doesn't mean that you should. In fact, if you're flying a real aircraft, you avoid those kinds of situations at all times, *unless* you received training as a stunt pilot and your aircraft was designed for stressful maneuvers.

REMEMBER

Making risky maneuvers without proper training, or while flying an aircraft not designed for such maneuvers, is a direct violation of this basic rule. Seems straightforward, right? It is, and so you should always match your training, experience, and aircraft to the flying activities that you undertake, whether you're flying physically or virtually.

>> **Never operate an aircraft so close to another aircraft that you create a possible collision hazard.** Regarding formation flying, don't operate an aircraft in formation flight unless you've arranged to do so with the pilots of the other aircraft in the formation.

>> **Always follow the right-of-way rules for surrounding air traffic.** Flying includes a number of right-of-way rules, but here are the basic ones:

- *In an emergency, an aircraft in distress has the right of way over all other types of air traffic.* You commonly find out about emergencies by radio, so listen up to surrounding radio channels and especially, to any warnings that you're in the path of the aircraft In distress.

- *When aircraft of the same type are converging at the same altitude, then the aircraft to the right has the right of way every time.* So, if you're flying an aircraft and you approach another aircraft from their right, you have the right of way. Determining your relative position can be a little confusing, but after you see it in action, you can understand it pretty easily. You steer clear of another plane's right of way by changing speed or heading.

» **No aircraft can operate below 10,000 feet mean sea level (MSL) at an airspeed of more than 250 knots.** That's roughly 288 miles per hour (mph). Going faster than this stated speed limit at altitudes below 10,000 feet (Figure 15-1 shows an airplane below this altitude) requires additional authorization by the air traffic control (ATC).

Also, know the speed limits for your specific aircraft and be aware of faster airplanes out there because they might quickly overtake you if you're on the same vector.

**FIGURE 15-1:**
Follow all airspeed regulations.

## Following the rules virtually

When it comes to flying virtually in Flight Simulator, you might be tempted to ignore the basic FARs. After all, this is just a video game, a simulation. Right? Definitely not. To get the most out of the simulation, you should abide by the basic rules whenever possible. You find a few game-related consequences of ignoring rules, but I encourage you to do your part and use your imagination to fill in the gaps between the game and real life.

In order to provide you with a realistic flight experience — perhaps including an authentic-looking airport terminal, as shown in Figure 15-2 — the simulator abides by the rules that real-world pilots have to follow when flying. Not only is the game designed around following basic aviation rules, but also the Flight Simulator online community deserves the respect shown when you follow these rules.

FIGURE 15-2:
The Flight
Simulator
world
incorporates
real-world
aviation
regulations
and facilities.

Airspeed rules, as well as right-of-way rules, all apply to your virtual flying, especially when playing in the game's online mode where you encounter other pilots and air traffic. You can engage these safety rules to avoid crashing in the game (perhaps by flying too fast) or otherwise putting your flights at risk.

# Knowing What Not to Do

For every list of rules that you should obey (see the section "Playing It Safe by Following the Rules," earlier in this chapter), you can find a list of warnings about what you shouldn't do. In this section, you can find a list of things you shouldn't ever do in traditional aviation, or in the virtual environment of Flight Simulator.

Keep these caveats in mind when you take a plane up in the virtual skies:

>> **Don't cut off other pilots.** Stay mindful of the other aircraft around you by regularly talking with ATC and by looking around for other traffic when flying by using Visual Flight Rules (VFR). Airplanes can be massive and, many times, may be flying Instrument Flight Rules (IFR) plans, meaning they use instruments alone — so they may not be scanning visually for other air traffic.

And, because you have so many airplanes up there, keep in constant check with ATC to avoid potentially adverse situations:

- *Overlapping flight paths:* Pilots often need to generate or change flight paths (like the one shown in Figure 15-3) based on weather, which often means that multiple aircraft are flying similar flight paths. This situation is ripe for encountering other air traffic, possibly on collision courses.

- *Waiting your turn in the line of aircraft:* Always avoid cutting off other pilots when you're taking off or landing; cutting others off creates a long list of potential issues, such as collisions and delays down the line.

**FIGURE 15-3:** Flight paths often need to change mid-flight due to weather and other factors.

>> **Don't spam the radio.** Pilots talk with ATC and get access to flight plan and other important information by using the radio. (See Chapter 14 for more information about using the radio to communicate with ATC.) Because communication with ATC is so crucial, always avoid spamming by making

needless radio transmissions on ATC channels when you don't actually need to get vital information. Spamming the radio cuts off access to ATC for other pilots and can also interfere if ATC is trying to get important information to you.

>> **Don't speed — ever.** Make sure that you abide by any air (and ground) speed regulations at any point. Adhering to the speed limit makes the flight more comfortable for your virtual passengers and helps ensure that you can land safely and smoothly when descending to an airport for arrival.

# 5

# What to Do in Case of an Emergency

**IN THIS PART . . .**

Discover how to recognize and deal with disastrous emergency situations that you can encounter during your Microsoft Flight Simulator 2020 flights — they do happen (and you can actually make them happen).

Find out how to prepare for and perform an emergency landing — at an airport or not — under various circumstances.

Chapter **16**

# Mayday! Recognizing and Responding to Emergencies

aking off and getting into the air in Microsoft Flight Simulator 2020 is a big part of the challenge for any flight. And sometimes takeoff can be the only part of the flight that presents any difficulty at all. But one intriguing feature that Flight Simulator offers is the option to set up multiple types of aircraft failures and schedule these failures for when you want them to occur. Planning an aircraft failure enables you to practice various emergency sequences, such as setting up for landing when your landing gear won't extend or even battling an engine fire.

Of course, you can run into a multitude of different emergencies while flying in Flight Simulator. And if you want to survive each one and keep your plane in the air — or land it safely when needed — you must know the characteristics of the emergency you're up against. In this chapter, I present different types of emergencies that you can encounter in the game, describe appropriate responses to each type, and explain how to adapt so that you can keep your plane on course.

# Yes, It's Probably an Emergency

Imagine that you're in the middle of a flight. You're making good time and getting ready to approach your next check-in waypoint. But something else is happening. Suddenly, lights begin to flash on the aircraft cockpit's control panel. You don't really know what these lights (which are glowing red in Figure 16-1) might mean, but you can tell something has gone wrong.

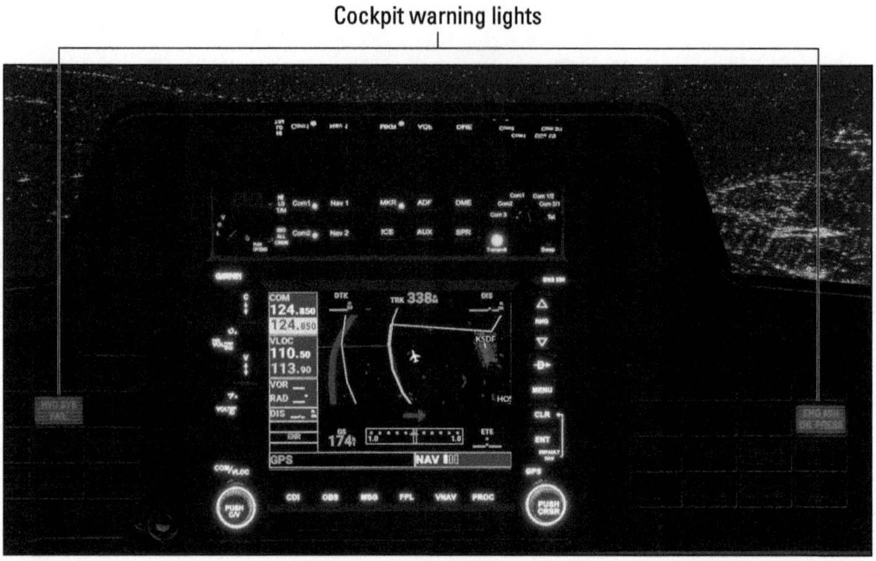

Cockpit warning lights

**FIGURE 16-1:** Heed the red lights in a dark cockpit.

If the flashing-light situation happens to you, then you're most likely dealing with an aircraft failure of some kind. You must think quickly to figure out exactly what that failure is because each kind of failure comes with its own challenges.

Table 16-1 outlines the types of failures that you can set up and schedule in Flight Simulator as of this guide's writing.

The exact failure options you see can change based on the aircraft that you're flying. However, you always get some variant of the failure options listed in Table 16-1. You can also initiate other types of failures, such as issues with the landing gear, in the flight options screen on the World Map menu to add additional challenge to your flight.

**TABLE 16-1**     **Aircraft Failures That You Can Choose**

| Failure | What It Simulates | How You Recognize It |
|---|---|---|
| Complete failure | Failure of all electrical and mechanical systems that power and control the aircraft | Your engines and electronics shut down. You have no control over the aircraft. |
| Oil system failure | Electrical failure in the system that lubricates the aircraft engine with oil | RPMs drop and the engine eventually seizes and dies. |
| Oil leak | Mechanical failure that causes a leak in the oil system | A drop in oil pressure shown by your oil pressure gauge. Eventually leads to an oil system failure for the affected engine. |
| Fuel pump failure | Electrical or mechanical failure of the pump that delivers fuel to the aircraft engine | Fuel pressure gauge shows decreased or no pressure. Affected engine eventually dies. |
| Fire | Fire in one or more of the aircraft engines | Alert on the main cockpit display, a high-pitched alarm, and a blinking Fire button |
| Magneto left | Electrical failure in the aircraft's left magneto | RPMs decrease and engine runs rougher. |
| Magneto right | Electrical failure in the aircraft's right magneto | Same as above. |
| Cylinder or engine failure | Loss of power in a prop or jet engine | Engine immediately ceases functions and RPMs drop to 0. |

# Preparing for Emergency Scenarios

When an emergency situation hits, falling into panic mode can be a common reaction. *Note:* Panicking isn't going to keep your aircraft in the air. So plan ahead and make sure you're prepared for emergencies when you head into any flight. Here are some good practices for emergency preparedness:

>> **Know what to do during an emergency ahead of time.** Practice the steps that you need to take to deal with oil leaks, for example. And be ready to make the decision to perform an emergency landing if it comes to that. But if you experience only a minor failure and you come back from it — because you figure out how to address that failure ahead of time — you can save your flight.

>> **Fly aircraft that you're already familiar with when you plan to introduce a failure.** Doing so makes dealing with failures much easier. For example, if you've been flying smaller planes, such as the Cessna 152, and then swap to

something bigger, such as the A320neo Airbus, you can struggle to contend with an emergency issue that pops up during flight because of your lack of familiarity with the plane and its controls. Figure 16-2 shows the difference in complexity of the cockpit equipment and controls in these two airplanes.

If you do decide to swap aircraft, take these precautions:

- *Spend time on the ground familiarizing yourself with controls* for the fuel mixture, various engine toggle switches, and other important components that you may need to work with on-the-fly if an emergency strikes.

- *Know important information about the weight and balance of your current aircraft* — such as the center of gravity and what percentage of the plane's max rated weight you're carrying — to help you prepare for any emergencies or failures that you might encounter during a flight.

**FIGURE 16-2:** A Cessna 152 cockpit (top) versus a more complex Airbus A320neo cockpit (bottom).

**REMEMBER**

Always have solid knowledge of and familiarity with the aircraft you're flying, especially if you're planning a longer flight that requires more time in the sky.

# Getting Safely Through the Emergency

Just because an emergency strikes, your flight doesn't have to come to an end. Take a breath and then analyze the evidence in front of you. If the Engine Fire light is blinking, you know what you're dealing with and can take steps to put out the fire. (You can find the actual steps to put out a fire in the section "Extinguishing Engine Fires," later in this chapter.)

You can solve every problem that you run into while in the air in some way — even if the solution is to bring down your aircraft in an emergency landing earlier than you expected. See Chapter 17 for the lowdown on emergency landings.

Follow these general steps to address an emergency:

1.  **Identify the problem and assess the damage.**

    Look for the indicators that tell you what the emergency involves. Some aircraft failures have a warning indicator on the control panel that actually names the problem: For example, a red panel light with the correct label might illuminate when an engine has low oil pressure. Sometimes you need to rely on other controls and gauges to show the issue, such as in the case of an oil leak. The oil pressure gauge can show that fluid is escaping the system. Refer to Table 16-1 for how to identify various failures.

2.  **Perform the activities that you must do to address the problem and manage the damage that you identified.**

    The actual steps for addressing a flying emergency depend on the type and extent of the emergency.

3.  **With the initial emergency under control, decide the fate of your flight and plan what to do next.**

    Two main possibilities exist for the fate of your flight:

    -   *If the emergency issue wasn't anything major and you have it handled,* then you can easily continue on your flight. However, you may need to adapt some things, such as trimming to compensate for less power or increasing the throttle on one engine to make up for a loss of another.

• *If the emergency situation is bad enough that you can't continue your flight,* you must prepare for an emergency landing. See Chapter 17 for the lowdown on coming down in less-than-optimal circumstances.

## Adapting to continue your flight

Sometimes when you're flying in an emergency situation, you need to adapt to keep your aircraft in the air. For example, suppose you lose an engine and need to adjust because you're using just three engines on a four-engine aircraft. Or suppose you lose power to your single engine and need to let your aircraft glide until you can restart the engine.

You might even need to prepare for a non-standard landing at your intended arrival airport — without the landing gear down if it doesn't descend — by adapting your airport approach and your communications with air traffic control (ATC) to explain the situation.

**REMEMBER**

Additionally, it may sound harsh, but the ATC in-game doesn't actually respond — or care — if you have an emergency. Because you have no real way to declare an emergency, ATC won't divert you to an airfield that's close to you. You simply have to role-play these situations for yourself.

Figuring out how to adapt to out-of-the norm situations takes time and practice. For example, experiencing an engine fire means putting out the fire and deciding how to adapt your flight plans in the aftermath. You can

>> **Try to bring the engine back online** and, if successful, continue the flight to your planned destination. You can always leave the affected engine offline as well — unless it's the only one you have, of course. In real life, however, you don't want to restart an engine. Doing so risks reigniting the fire, and that's the primary thing you want to avoid.

>> **Deal with the engine being dead** for the rest of the flight. When you have multiple engines, you may continue the flight, but with slower airspeed and a behind-schedule landing.

**REMEMBER**

Familiarity with your aircraft is essential. Whether you can accept a dead engine and continue the flight depends on characteristics of the airplane itself and the range to your destination.

# Knowing when to call it and land early

Any type of emergency may call for putting down an aircraft before the flight is scheduled to be over, which you can find disheartening. Chapter 17 offers specifics on making emergency landings, but in this chapter, I present the kinds of failures and emergencies that might dictate an early end to your flight.

Examples of flight-ending scenarios include engine failure (depicted in Figure 16-3), engine fires, and even smaller issues such as oil leaks. Or you may experience multiple failures that stack up on you and end the flight because you just can't deal with them all quickly enough.

Engine failure!

**FIGURE 16-3:** Engine failure can keep a plane from making it to its destination.

**TIP**

When you're flying high in the skies as the pilot in command, only you can make the call to abort a flight. The ultimate line in the sand for determining when to throw in the towel (so to speak) is the answer to the following question:

How difficult will it be to get this aircraft to my destination?

If the answer to that question is *too difficult* or even *impossible,* then seriously consider looking for emergency landing opportunities. Depending on what kind of flight you're making (IFR or VFR, which I talk about in Chapter 11), this landing may involve finding a nearby airport that can slot you in or even landing in the middle of nowhere (see Figure 16-4).

FIGURE 16-4:
Making an
emergency
landing in a
field.

# Dealing with Equipment Failures

Aircraft are essentially just massive machines that have computers running them, and they're bound to run into technical problems at some point. These technical problems can be electrical or mechanical failures, as simple as losing one system's function, or as detrimental as losing power to your entire aircraft. No matter what type of failure you run into, knowing how to react — and being able to react quickly — can mean the difference between safely landing your aircraft or crashing into a forest in the middle of nowhere.

## Acting on electrical failures

Aircraft have a myriad of possible electrical issues that you can run into. These issues range from the flaps not responding to their controls, to the battery dying or your plane's alternator not enabling an engine to restart.

REMEMBER

For some electrical failures, you may be able to reset certain systems or simply navigate without those systems — for example, if the GPS system (which includes your digital navigation) goes out in your aircraft, you can fly without it. In the event of a more serious failure — such as when the flaps stop responding or the battery dies — then you need to land the aircraft as quickly as possible. When responding to a serious event, keep a cool head and focus on the solution (see the section "Preparing for Emergency Scenarios," earlier in this chapter, for the general steps to approaching an emergency).

If your plane has a serious electrical failure, look for emergency landing zones in preferably flat, open areas. I introduce what kind of areas to keep an eye out for, and even what to do to perform an emergency landing, in Chapter 17.

## Responding to engine failures

Engine failure occurs when one (or more than one — or all) of the aircraft's engines give out and fail to function in the way that they should do to propel the aircraft. You know that an engine gives out when it drops to 0 RPM and doesn't respond to the throttle.

Engines can give out for a number of reasons: problems with the *fuel mixture* (the ratio of oxygen and aviation fuel that provides efficient combustion), an issue with the fuel line or lines, or even a mechanical problem with the engine that you can't fix while in the air.

When an engine fails, immediate effects on the aircraft can include

>> A drop in speed

>> Loss of power generation (battery only)

>> Loss of maneuverability

Follow these steps when an engine failure occurs to counteract the adverse effects on the aircraft:

1. **Situate your aircraft so that it maintains its current airspeed.**

   You maintain airspeed by adjusting pitch. With no thrust, you'll have to constantly trade altitude for speed to keep the plane from stalling.

2. **Try to restart the engine by pulling the throttle back and then pushing it forward again.**

   - *From a PC keyboard,* you can use the function keys F1, F2, and F3 to control the throttle (see more keyboard controls in Chapter 2).

   - *On an Xbox controller,* press A to increase the throttle and B to decrease it.

   In real life, this pull-and-push action is called *cycling the throttle,* and it can sometimes kick the engine back on. However, Flight Simulator doesn't model this cycling in every plane.

3. **If cycling the throttle doesn't work, reset the fuel mixture by interacting directly with the mix panel.**

   The mix panel's appearance and location can vary based on the type of aircraft that you're flying and its cockpit design.

If resetting the mixture doesn't bring the engine back to life and you have no other engines, then call it and correct course for a nearby airport or find another emergency landing zone where you can set down.

If you have other engines, you can often complete your flight like normal, although you may need to pay a bit more attention to the controls throughout the flight. Keep in mind that loss of an engine in real life would always result in an emergency diversion. However, because ATC won't acknowledge any damage to your plane in Flight Simulator, you can make the call for this situation.

# Extinguishing Engine Fires

When piloting your virtual plane, you can potentially run into engine fires, which are dangerous and can often lead to crashes and even complete engine failure if you don't deal with them quickly. You can usually recognize an engine fire easily because your cockpit warns you with lights that flash (see Figure 16-5) and audible alarms (refer to Table 16-1). Unfortunately, aircraft in Flight Simulator don't all have the same fire deterrent systems, and not all planes have them in the first place. Dealing with engine fires takes practice and solid knowledge of the aircraft that you're flying.

**FIGURE 16-5:**
Engine fires are accompanied by flashing lights and blaring alerts.

**TIP**

If you plan to run flight scenarios in an aircraft that's equipped with the Engine Fires failure — and it's turned on — get acquainted with the cockpit of the aircraft that you're flying. Know where to look for each step of the process to address the fire.

## Using your aircraft's fire deterrent system (if available)

When you're flying an aircraft and experience an engine fire, respond quickly by following these steps:

1. **Pull the engine throttle back to idle.**

   - *From a PC keyboard,* you can use F2 to decrease the throttle.

   - *On an Xbox controller,* press B to decrease throttle.

   This action cuts a lot of the fuel intake to the engine.

2. **Locate the Engine Fire push button for the affected engine.**

   Aircraft that have multiple engines have multiple engine buttons, each labeled for the engine that it corresponds to — Engine 1, Engine 2, and so on.

3. **Activate the fire control sequence.**

   How this works depends on the plane you're currently flying. Most of the time, you just have to remove a guard (if one is installed) and then push or hold the button. However, not all planes have fire suppression systems modeled.

   Some planes may have further fire control systems that require multiple steps. Familiarize yourself with your aircraft before taking off and ensure you understand what steps need to be performed in case of fire. After the initial fire suppression agent has been disbursed, you may have to follow up with another action depending on your aircraft model.

**WARNING**

   If you don't wait for the fire suppression agent to complete and for the engine to fully power it down then attempts to fight the fire can prove ineffective because fuel is still being pumped into the engine, As a result, the fire may continue to burn or even spread.

4. **Check the fuel system for leaks by locating the fuel pressure readout on your cockpit's dashboard.**

   Some cockpits may utilize analog systems rather than digital panels.

**WARNING**

   If you're running an aircraft that doesn't have multiple engines, then a fuel leak means that you absolutely must perform an emergency landing because it's only a matter of time before your (likely) damaged single engine dies.

5. **Ensure you're not leaking fuel by checking that fuel pressure is stable and your craft is consuming the proper amount of fuel.**

   If the fuel lines appear secure, then you can try to restart the engine. However, restarting the engine might kickstart the fire back into play and cause even more issues. The following section goes into what to do after you extinguish the fire.

**REMEMBER**

The procedure outlined in the preceding steps is by no means a one-size-fits-all scenario. The cockpit design and layout of all the buttons and systems can vary with each aircraft. Before you even get off the ground, take note of your aircraft's fire deterrent systems and the steps that you need to follow to put out an engine fire.

# Deciding what to do after the fire is out

After you put out the engine fire (which I talk about in the preceding section), you need to make some evaluations and decisions regarding your next steps. You can

» **Avoid attempting to restart the engine.** Most fire suppression systems cut off all fuel, fluids, and power to an engine, so this isn't really a choice. However, if you were flying an aircraft without a fire suppression system and shut a burning engine down, attempting to restart it might reignite the fire.

» **Evaluate whether you can complete your flight at reduced power.** If you're flying an aircraft that has multiple engines and decide not to try restarting the engine that had the fire, you might be able to continue your flight as planned, knowing that you'll arrive late. Again, in real life, unless it's a short distance to your destination, any engine loss is enough of an emergency to require a diversion to a closer airport.

» **Turn to a nearby airport and set down your flight,** which is probably the best option if you experience fuel leakage.

# Chapter **17**

# Making an Emergency Landing

hapter 16 gives you an idea about what types of emergency situations you might encounter in Microsoft Flight Simulator 2020 and how to prepare for, identify, and respond to them. But despite your best efforts, you may find yourself in an emergency situation that you just can't fix. Suppose that you can't put out that engine fire, or your nerves are just too far gone to keep flying.

While the game does not feature many provisions for actual emergency scenarios, there are important things you must remember about tackling what is there so you're not dealing with frustrating endgame sequences.

So when an unmanageable emergency happens, you must start looking for a nearby place to put down your aircraft. This is called an *emergency landing*, and in this chapter, I explain how to handle an emergency landing in Flight Simulator.

## THE CURRENT STATE OF EMERGENCY LANDINGS IN FLIGHT SIMULATOR

**REMEMBER**

Flight Simulator's emergency landings are quirky:

- **The game counts any landing outside of an airport as a crash.** So you can't technically complete an emergency landing off-runway — at least, not by the game's standards. If the emergency is dire, though, you may need to attempt a landing on roads, in clearings, or even in the water.

- **Just because the game doesn't count a landing outside an airport as successful doesn't mean that you can't do it.** But to maintain your spotless, no-crash flying record, focus your efforts on making it to an airport before trying to land.

I believe that it's most likely only a matter of time until mods or other third-party content, which you can incorporate into Flight Simulator play, makes emergency landing outside of airport limits a more game-friendly solution. Until then, though, be aware of the current airport-only limitation.

# Strategizing and Practicing for Emergency Landings

Be prepared for an emergency landing at any point during a flight; this vigilance can make all the difference in the world. Study various emergency scenarios (see Chapter 16) and get to know the controls of your aircraft that can help you recognize, respond to, and manage an emergency. Even if your flight is going smoothly at first, you never know when an engine — or two — might go out and you have to land your aircraft in the middle of the rural United States.

*Note:* Flight Simulator is a bit lacking in detail when it comes to emergency situations. For example, you find that many airplanes don't actually have fire extinguishing systems modeled, and so, these systems can't be of use when practicing procedures to put out an engine fire.

**REMEMBER**

Figuring out how to deal successfully with emergencies and emergency landings requires you to play through the same scenarios repeatedly. You can easily get this practice, though, especially when you know the scenarios that you want to master. Just keep working on your chosen emergencies and use everything you know — your aircraft controls, your flight path and surroundings, and emergency process steps — to your advantage.

These points can help you with preparation for a possible emergency landing and smooth execution of the landing if you need it:

>> **Keep an eye out for locations that could work as good emergency landing zones along your route, even when an emergency doesn't yet exist.** This awareness of your surroundings and waypoints along your flight path helps you quickly choose possible landing areas in case something actually goes wrong.

>> **Be studious and mindful of your aircraft's characteristics and capabilities.** Related information includes your cruising airspeed, weight distribution, the number and status of your engines (and whether your airplane can continue flying with only one of two engines, for example), whether your landing gear is stationary or retractable, status of the plane's flight control surfaces, how far you can stretch your fuel supply, and so on. If you're having issues with retractable landing gear that won't deploy, for example, you need to approach an emergency landing slower than you would if the landing gear is working perfectly.

# Determining a Landing Location

Gearing up for an emergency landing in Flight Simulator involves following two primary steps:

1. **Deal with the situation that led to the emergency.**

   Emergencies include situations such as engine fires, fuel mixture issues, electrical failures, and even hydraulic or other mechanical problems. (See possible cockpit warning lights in Figure 17-1 and also the information on identifying and handling emergency situations in Chapter 16.) Each situation affects the type of emergency landing you need to perform (whether it's gliding to a stop or doing a belly landing, for example) because each issue can change how long you can keep your aircraft in the sky.

TIP

   Your imagination is your greatest ally for confronting emergencies in Flight Simulator. In a real-life situation, ATC would normally divert your flight to an emergency landing location. But because Flight Simulator offers no way in-game to declare an emergency, you must simply be a bit creative and imagine your landing solution.

**FIGURE 17-1:**
You never
know when
your cockpit
display might
signal an
emergency.

**2.** **Target and head for a nearby airport (preferably) or a flat, clear area near your flight path where you can potentially land the airplane.**

Finding a location to land depends on various factors such as

- *Where you are in the progress along your flight path:* If you're close to an airport or can continue the flight long enough to make it to one, then you obviously want to go for that option. However, an airport might not be nearby. In some situations, you may need to find an emergency landing zone in the middle of nowhere.

- *What kind of terrain surrounds you:* The best types of off-runway emergency landing zones include a lot of flat area. You might find a valley between two mountains, or even a back country road without a lot of traffic. You might also target a field behind someone's house, as shown in Figure 17-2.

- *The size and condition of your airplane and the makeshift runway:* Look for a location that fits the size of your aircraft, both widthwise and lengthwise. You need enough width to avoid crashing into obstructions (such as trees or buildings) and enough length to offer plenty of time to slow down the aircraft — again, to avoid crashing into anything. In a lot of instances, if you're flying an international flight across an ocean, you may need to rely on landing in the water, especially if you don't have the engine power to get to your destination.

**FIGURE 17-2:**
Don't look for a
perfect
emergency
landing zone; a
field can work
in a pinch.

**WARNING**

Performing an emergency landing outside of an airport results in a crash and a failed flight, according to Flight Simulator. However, if you're close enough to an airport to land successfully, you need to speak with air traffic control (ATC) so that they can assign you a runway and hopefully offer other helpful instructions. Unfortunately, Flight Simulator's emergency landing systems aren't well simulated (pilots, use your imagination!), so you just need to ask for a runway and then do your best to set up your own approach.

# Adjusting the Approach and Touching Down

After you establish a location to land, it's time to perform your emergency landing. Like you do for any landing, start by dropping down and aligning the aircraft with the target landing area — whether it's a runway assigned by ATC at an airport, or a flat area chosen from the surrounding landscape.

The runway approach in an emergency landing process is much like the approach for a normal landing (get the scoop on normal approach and landing in Chapter 9), except you may need to change some approach characteristics based on your engine speed and other aircraft capabilities:

>> **Evaluate your airspeed and engine power.** Suppose you're flying a twin engine plane and lose the use of one engine (see Figure 17-3). You may not have sufficient engine power left over to maintain a normal airspeed and pitch on approach. In this case, coming in for landing from a higher altitude gives you a greater chance of landing successfully since you have longer to line up with your target and bleed off speed.

**FIGURE 17-3:**
Approaching an emergency landing zone requires precision and patience.

>> **Consider how to time your approach and adjust for the actual touch-down spot carefully.** If your landing gear is down and functioning, then approach as normal, touching down about one-third of the way down the runway. However, if hydraulic issues have kept you from being able to extend the landing gear, you're going to need to belly slide the aircraft to a halt, so land closer to the near end of the runway. What type of aircraft you're flying determines how easy or difficult this maneuver is — you can more easily stop a smaller, single-engine aircraft (such as a Cessna 172) than a jumbo jet (such as a Boeing 787), because the single-engine plane has a lower stall speed and less mass.

**REMEMBER**

If you're not landing on a normal runway, you just need to touch down, and the game automatically counts your landing as a crash. As such, you don't have to worry about getting the landing pitch perfect the first time. You can always run another scenario and play out the emergency landing until you perfect it.

# Making a Power-Off Approach

If your emergency results from a total power failure, you may need to worry about making a *power-off approach*. This dire emergency means that you've lost all electrical power and have no access to any instrumentation or functionality that requires power. Analog systems may work, but functionality will likely be degraded. This kind of emergency landing can be especially tricky because you can't contact ATC or speak with anyone else about the landing.

When this situation happens, you must make the most of the airspeed you've already established. Making a successful approach and landing with no power means staying at a higher altitude and using your aircraft's glide capability to get as far as you need to in order to hit your target landing zone. To help maintain the airspeed and glide path, you need to keep your aircraft's nose level with the horizon as much as possible. You may have to trade altitude for speed now and then to avoid stalling, but you want to keep your descent shallow and controlled.

## Seeing without seeing

Because a power-off approach takes away the use of your instruments, you need to figure out how to see your path without seeing it through the instruments. This ability is especially important during night flights, when the sky and ground can really blend together.

The idea of seeing without seeing might seem silly, but it's actually a skill that many pilots develop in real flight. Under Visual Flight Rules (VFR) conditions with good visibility, you rely on your eyes during a normal flight. But without your instruments, you have to estimate where things are based on how the shadows and outlines look, as shown in Figure 17-4.

**FIGURE 17-4:**
Outlines can tell you where landmarks and obstacles are, even in the dark.

Your night flight still might end in a crash the first few times, but after a few practice scenarios, you can more clearly distinguish the terrain around you, even at night.

## Using your navigational sense

In addition to helping you use only your eyes to see (no instruments), honing your navigational sense can help you maintain your flight path. Using your *navigational sense* means making the most of your navigational markers, such as

>> **Landmarks (rivers, mountains, and large structures):** When you recognize landmarks on your flight, you can use them to tell whether you're heading in the right direction.

>> **The location of the sun:** Paying attention to where the sun is located in the sky and its position relative to the horizon can also help you figure out in which direction you're heading.

# 6

# The Part of Tens

Chapter **18**

# Ten Flight Simulator Tricks You Should Know

Like real-world flying, Microsoft Flight Simulator 2020 has a seemingly never-ending bag of tricks. Despite being an incredibly realistic sim, don't forget that Flight Simulator is also a game — and there are *always* secrets and hints in games.

Luckily, you don't need official pilot credentials (or 1,500 flight hours of experience) to figure out intriguing ways to energize soaring through the sky with Flight Simulator. Whether you're looking for a way to skip a complicated takeoff sequence (and get right to the good part) or how to quickly refuel your aircraft, I've gathered cool (and useful!) ways for you to make Flight Simulator just what you want it to be.

The tips in this chapter can make hopping into the cockpit and exploring the virtual world a little easier for beginners — and maybe even a bit more fun, too! But they're not just for beginners; even a seasoned Flight Simulator veteran might find these tricks absolutely worth retaining, *especially* if you plan to play the game for many moons to come.

# Start in Midair

Did you know you can completely skip the takeoff sequence? It's true, and you may prefer starting in midair if you want to (initially) avoid what can be a lengthy learning experience. Getting a plane into the air can be an intimidating and frustrating experience (even when you have this For Dummies guide at hand), and some potential players may give up before they even get in the air.

Unless you're a hands-on learner — or find the prospect of figuring things out while flying blind exciting — a craft full of confusing buttons and levers can be scary. Perhaps you want to omit takeoff and just concentrate on the simpler and more relaxing experience of flying the plane in the air.

**REMEMBER**

Avoiding the takeoff sequence is a trick you might want to employ if you don't care about making your flights as realistic as possible. If you want to figure out all the ins and outs of flying a plane, however, you might not want to employ this tip because takeoff is an important part of becoming a pilot, virtual or otherwise.

To start your flights already in midair, follow these steps:

1. **Go to the World Map.**

   See Chapter 3 for info on the World Map.

2. **Left-click or press A anywhere on the World Map that isn't an airport.**

3. **Choose the Set As Departure option from the pop-up menu shown in Figure 18-1.**

4. **Press the Fly button in the lower right of the screen to start your flight.**

When you complete these steps, you can begin your journey at around 1,500 feet in the air. Doing so enables you to continue flying from there without concerning yourself with a complicated takeoff checklist. You won't need to worry about learning the fundamentals of flight — at least, not how to use your throttle controls or anything much more complicated than how to keep your craft in the air.

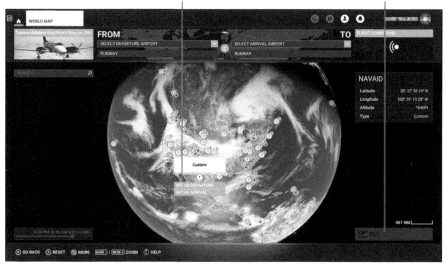

Set departure from the World Map          Fly button

FIGURE 18-1:
Choosing a
departure
point for
starting your
flight in midair.

# Find Animals Quickly

If you've already flown across the globe looking for special landmarks (or even your house), you've probably thought about getting a closer look at some of the animals that call Earth home, too. But finding them can often be a little like looking for a needle in a haystack (outside of zoos and other animal sanctuaries).

How do you find animals so that you can get up close and personal? You can actually seek them out in a very simple way, and it only takes a few seconds. Follow these steps to get all the animal experiences you crave:

1. **Go to the World Map.**

2. **Type the word** fauna **in the search bar (found on the left side of the screen) and click the Search icon.**

   A long list of animals appears, telling you where you can find them in the game, as shown in Figure 18-2.

3. **Click to choose your next destination from the list of locations that feature animals.**

4. **After you start your flight and you're on your way to the chosen destination, access the Pause menu by pressing Escape or the Menu button.**

5. **Click the Assistance tab.**

6. **Click the Navigation menu and find the Fauna Markers option.**

7. **Click to toggle on the option.**

   Markers appear on the map to show where you can find animals along your route.

You need to decide which animals you want to find, but with Fauna Markers turned on, this decision becomes less of a headache. You may even decide you want to start running animal tours the next time you jump into Flight Simulator.

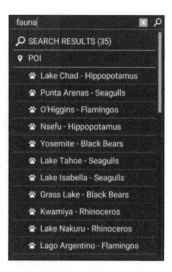

fauna

SEARCH RESULTS (35)

POI

Lake Chad - Hippopotamus
Punta Arenas - Seagulls
O'Higgins - Flamingos
Nsefu - Hippopotamus
Yosemite - Black Bears
Lake Tahoe - Seagulls
Lake Isabella - Seagulls
Grass Lake - Black Bears
Kwamiya - Rhinoceros
Lake Nakuru - Rhinoceros
Lago Argentino - Flamingos

**FIGURE 18-2:**
Locating fauna in the world.

# Refuel Your Aircraft Anywhere

When you take a lengthy flight in real life, you probably wonder how such massive aircraft travel long distances without the need to stop and refuel. Although many planes have the capability to refuel in midair, this typically doesn't occur in the real world — outside of emergencies. But in Flight Simulator, you can refuel while flying without missing a beat. You just need to change your keybindings (options that are tied to a specific input device key or key combination; see Chapter 2), but that change doesn't take very long. Just follow these steps:

1. **Access the Pause Menu and click the Controls tab.**

2. **In the Controls Options window that appears, choose the input type that you're using.**

   You can choose from Keyboard, Mouse, or Controller.

   TIP

   If you're playing on an Xbox console, you're likely playing with a controller.

3. **Scroll down the resulting list of options and select the Repair and Refuel keybinding option.**

   If you don't want to scroll, you can type **Repair and Refuel** in the search bar in the left column of the Controls Options window, as shown in Figure 18-3.

4. **Choose a key on your input device to which you want to bind the Repair and Refuel option.**

5. **Press escape or the Menu button to exit the Pause menu screen.**

After you follow the preceding steps, you should still be in midair. You can press the key you just selected to instantly repair any issues with your aircraft that might be plaguing you at present, as well as receive an automatic refueling. You don't need to do anything special after that. Your gas gauge should be full once more!

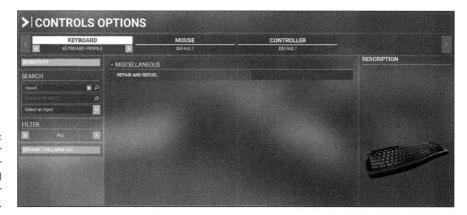

FIGURE 18-3:
Searching for the Repair and Refuel option for key-binding.

**REMEMBER**

Alternatively, you can skip the keybinding refueling scenario and simply turn on the Unlimited Fuel option in the Assistance settings in the Pause menu. With unlimited fuel toggled on, you never have to worry about those fuel-guzzling planes running out of their go juice while in the air.

# Turn Off Satellite Overlay

The Flight Simulator's World Map has a lot of information to keep track of. And you may have a little difficulty finding certain landmarks when you use the World Map's default view (which is a satellite photo). The default view is great at showing terrain and cities but might be a bit overwhelming for people who are used to political maps.

You can toggle on an IFR view that may mitigate potential issues with locating landmarks. When you use IFR view, you get a plain gray map that makes it a lot easier to see things like distance between points at a glance.

To turn on IFR view in the World Map, follow these steps:

1. **From the main screen open the World Map.**

2. **Choose the Open Filters option that appears in the shortcut bar in the lower part of your screen.**

   A window appears, as shown in Figure 18-4, where you can scroll through filter options.

3. **Click the arrows to the left and right of the Background Map option to toggle the IFR option to replace Satellite.**

After following the preceding steps, you should have a better, more granular view of the Earth below.

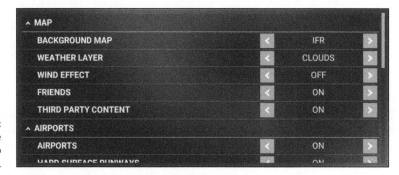

**FIGURE 18-4:**
Setting the
World Map to
IFR view.

# Explore Outside the Plane

Did you know you can leave the plane in midair to look at the world around you? No, you aren't physically exiting the plane. But using a feature called *Active Pause*, you can take a look at your surroundings without having to land.

Active Pause stops your plane right where it is, and you can explore your aircraft's cockpit, immediate surroundings in the air, or the entire world around you. Here's how to turn on Active Pause:

1. **Press Escape or the Menu button to go to the Pause menu, click on options, and click on the Assistance menu, which is shown in Figure 18-5.**

2. **Look for the Play/Pause icon on the toolbar that appears when you hover the mouse near the top of your screen.**

   This icon represents a toggle for Active Pause.

3. **Click the Play/Pause icon to activate the Active Pause play mode.**

   Toggling on the Active Pause mode activates a drone that you can maneuver using the standard aircraft controls on the keyboard or controller. You can explore to your heart's content without ruining your flight. And you don't even have to stop playing to do it!

Pause/Play icon

FIGURE 18-5:
Look around
your flight path
by using the
Active Pause
mode.

# Explore the Streets

You may be playing a flight sim, but you still have plenty of ways to interact with the world around you. The same drone that allows you to exit the cockpit and travel around the world (during an Active Pause; see the preceding section) enables you to travel down to the streets and have a look around. It may take a bit of doing because your plane is fairly high up in the sky, but you absolutely can take your drone down to the streets (see Figure 18-6).

FIGURE 18-6:
Looking at
the world via
the Flight
Simulator
street view.

Your drone can give you a close-up look at buildings, flora and fauna, and landmarks around the Earth. The illustrations at street level don't look as sharp as the rest of the game, given the somewhat low-resolution imaging used to populate the locations, but you still get a close-up (if somewhat pixelated) look at whatever you want to see.

# Speed Up Your Flight

The flight paths you take in Flight Simulator run in real time. If you want to fly from California to Tokyo, you're going to have to wait out the 12 hours it takes in the real world to get there. Luckily, the game doesn't really force anyone to sit at their computer or TV for half a day to see cool new destinations. You have an easy solution: speeding up your flight.

You can speed up the game's *sim rate* (the rate at which your flight proceeds along its route) in order to reach your destination more quickly. You can also fly to your endpoint more slowly if you want. You can adjust the sim rate up and down at your leisure.

Follow these steps to adjust your game's sim rate if you're playing on a PC:

1. **Press the R key on your keyboard.**

2. **Hold the CTRL key and press either the plus (+) key or the minus (–) key on the number pad.**

   As I'm sure you can guess, pressing + speeds up the sim rate and pressing – slows it down.

Follow these steps to set your sim rate if you're playing on a console:

1. **Press Escape or the Menu button to go to the Pause menu, select Options, and select Controls Options.**

   From the Controls Options screen, as shown in Figure 18-7, you need to assign a button for the sim rate.

2. **Type the search term** sim rate **in the search box on the left side of the Controls Options window, and then click the Search icon.**

3. **Click to select the Sim Rate option.**

4. **When prompted, choose a key or console button when prompted that you want to bind to your Sim Rate option.**

After following the preceding steps, you can adjust the sim rate on your console easily:

» **Slow down:** Press your chosen button and the left trigger.

» **Speed up:** Press your chosen button and the right trigger.

By adjusting your sim rate, you can take those cross-country (or across-the-globe) flights in record time.

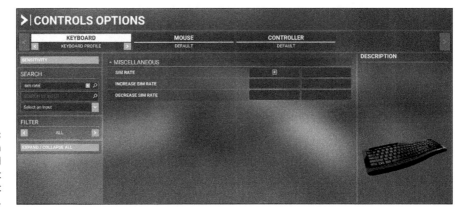

**FIGURE 18-7:**
Bind a keyboard button so that you can adjust sim rates.

# Fast Travel to Flight Phases

If you don't care much for the lengthy cruise phase of a flight, you might opt to skip it entirely. You can do that. Instead of actively flying through the entire trip, you can fast travel to a phase that's more appealing to you. To use the Travel To option, just follow these steps:

1. **Press Escape or the Menu button to open your Pause menu.**

2. **Click the Travel To button (which looks similar to a fast-forward button, as noted in Figure 18-8) to reveal your Travel To options.**

   The Travel To window that appears lists the phases of your flight plan that you can choose from. Figure 18-8 lists Cruise, Descent, Approach, Final, and Taxi.

3. **Select the phase to which you want to fast travel.**

   After you make your selection, your game skips to that phase.

Hate taking off or cruising? Use this trick to skip past all of it!

Travel To button

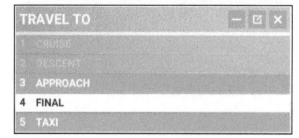

**FIGURE 18-8:** Finding your fast travel options in the Travel To window.

# Customize Your Pilot Avatar

You're more than just your plane in Flight Simulator. You have a pilot avatar, too! You might not see your avatar much while playing the game (your view is as the avatar in the cockpit), but you do have a character that represents you. Plus, you can change what your avatar looks like.

To customize your pilot avatar, follow these steps:

1. **Press Escape or the Menu button to open the Pause menu.**

2. **Click Options and then General.**

3. **In the General Options window that appears, click the Misc tab on the left.**

4. **Under Pilot Avatar Settings, repeatedly click the forward or backward arrow beside the Pilot Avatar to scroll through your options.**

   You can choose from 24 different pilot models. Find the one that suits you.

   The models appear on the right side of the General Options window, as shown in Figure 18-9.

5. **When you find the avatar that matches your mood today, select it by making your choices and leaving the Misc menu.**

Now you can have a pilot that (hopefully) better represents you in the virtual world!

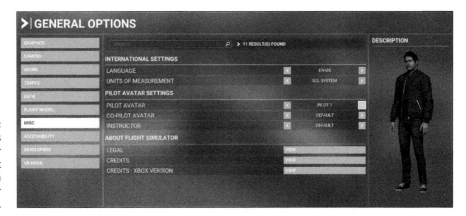

**FIGURE 18-9:** The various options for your pilot avatar in Pilot Avatar Settings.

# Change Your ATC Call Sign

Communicating with air traffic controllers (ATCs) is one of the more entertaining aspects of Flight Simulator. You need to maintain comms with ATC for a successful flight in-game (and in the real world). But you can have some fun with it, too.

You can actually change your *call sign*, or title, that the air traffic control team uses to identify and address you over the radio. Follow these steps to customize your call sign:

1. **Press Escape or the Menu button to go to the Pause menu.**

2. **Select the correct option to go to the World Map.**

3. **Choose ATC Options by clicking on your airplane in the upper left part of the screen, then select Customization from the menu on the left column.**

4. **In the text box next to Call Sign (see Figure 18-10), type in your desired call sign.**

   For example, perhaps you'd like to be known as 8675309.

   Choose a fun call sign, but don't be naughty. The game doesn't recognize profanity, so keep it G-rated (or you may be banned from online play).

   REMEMBER

5. **Save your choice by leaving the menu and return to your game.**

After you complete the preceding steps, ATC calls you by your desired call sign.

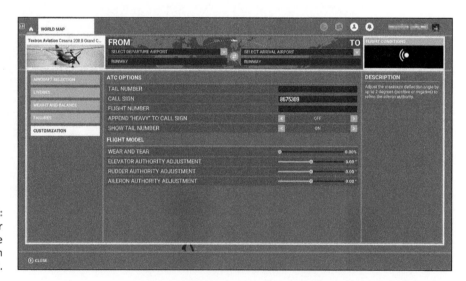

**FIGURE 18-10:**
Changing your call sign in the Customization window.

Chapter **19**

# Ten Cool Airports to Visit Virtually

ost people see air travel as a way to go from one place to another. Although you can see some amazing things on the way, where you start and where you end up are just as important. When making a flight plan, you must select your arrival and departure airports (unless you start in mid-flight) because you need to know where you'll take off and where you'll land. All other choices are secondary.

Fortunately, Microsoft Flight Simulator 2020 enables you to (virtually) check out almost every airport in the world. The selections in this chapter take you around the globe to visit facilities of every sort; a mixture of challenging and unique airports that you don't want to miss.

**REMEMBER**

For each airport in the chapter, I include a mini table that outlines its specifications. For the sake of keeping these specs short, I use abbreviations (*m* for meter and *ft* for foot, for example) and coordinate notations such as ° for degrees, ' for minutes, and " for seconds. Also, I use acronyms for airport codes — IATA for International Air Transport Association, and ICAO for International Civil Aviation Organization.

# Courchevel Altiport; French Alps

You can find Courchevel Altiport, shown in Figure 19-1, nestled in the French Alps. This facility services the nearby Courchevel ski resort and is surrounded by one of the most beautiful mountain ranges in the world. Unfortunately, this natural splendor also makes the airport one of the most dangerous a pilot can face.

FIGURE 19-1:
Courchevel
Altiport.

Courchevel Altiport has one very short runway (537 m/1,762 ft). Luckily, the 18.6-percent grade of the runway helps make up for the short runway in both landing and takeoff. In addition to the terrifying runway, the facility has no instrument approach procedure, no go-around procedure, or even lighting aids, which makes landing here at night practically impossible (see Chapter 9).

For a challenge and a beautiful environment, few airports in the world can beat out this one.

| Specification | Value |
| --- | --- |
| Year opened | 1962 |
| Airport type | Public |
| Airport codes | IATA: CVF |
| | ICAO: LFLJ |

| Specification | Value |
| --- | --- |
| Elevation | 2,008 m/6,588 ft |
| Coordinates | 45°23′51″N |
| | 06°38′04″E |

# Dubai International Airport; Dubai, United Arab Emirates

Dubai International is the busiest airport in the world when it comes to international passenger traffic, and it generates over 25 percent of Dubai's gross domestic product (both directly and indirectly). Started in 1960 as a small facility that had one compacted sand runway, this airport has grown in scale with its surroundings. And now this sprawling facility represents the economic prosperity that has transformed a small fishing village into a modern metropolis. Figure 19-2 shows the Dubai International Airport.

FIGURE 19-2:
Dubai
International
Airport.

Flying into Dubai, pilots can spot the tallest building in the world, the Burj Khalifa, and the beautiful blue waters of the Persian Gulf. The long runways, large facilities, and forgiving flight paths make this airport a great destination for airliners.

| Specification | Value |
| --- | --- |
| Year opened | 1960 |
| Airport type | Public |
| Airport codes | IATA: DXB |
| | ICAO: OMDB |
| Elevation | 19 m/62 ft |
| Coordinates | 25°15'10"N |
| | 055°21'52"E |

# Gustaf III Airport; St. Jean, Saint Barthélemy

Gustaf III Airport, shown in Figure 19-3, services the beautiful Caribbean island of Saint Barthélemy. Unfortunately, unlike its surroundings, taking off and landing at this airport is anything but lovely. On one side of the single runway, you have a steep hill that has a traffic circle at its crown. On the other, you have a public beach leading into a bay. Standing on the opposite side of the bay is a large mountain range.

The awkwardness of Gustaf III Airport's layout would be funny if it weren't so dangerous. But this airport's difficult configuration offers a great place to test your takeoff and landing skills (in the world of Flight Simulator, at least), and in this area, you can do some great sightseeing.

| Specification | Value |
| --- | --- |
| Year opened | 1984 |
| Airport type | Public |
| Airport codes | IATA: SBH |
| | ICAO: TFFJ |
| Elevation | 15 m/48 ft |

| Specification | Value |
| --- | --- |
| Coordinates | 17°54'16"N |
| | 062°50'38"W |

FIGURE 19-3:
Gustaf III
Airport.

# John F. Kennedy International Airport; New York City, New York, USA

Originally named New York International Airport, Anderson Field, this airport in the Big Apple is the busiest international air passenger gateway into North America. John F. Kennedy International Airport is a great airport to experience now because it's currently undergoing massive renovations. After they're completed, you can compare the new layout to the old to get a good idea of how terminals evolve over time. Getting to check out the Manhattan skyline and acquainting yourself with some of the world's highest-trafficked terminals make this airport worth visiting often. See Figure 19-4.

| Specification | Value |
| --- | --- |
| Year opened | 1948 |
| Airport type | Public |
| Airport codes | IATA: JFK |

| Specification | Value |
| --- | --- |
|  | ICAO: KJFK |
| Elevation | 4 m/13 ft |
| Coordinates | 40°38'23"N |
|  | 073°46'44"W |

# Juancho E. Yrausquin Airport; Saba, Lesser Antilles

Dubai International and JFK International (discussed in their own sections earlier in this chapter) are both large airports, but now I want to show you the smallest airport — in the world. With a runway that's only 400 meters (1,312 ft) long, Juancho E. Yrausquin Airport (see Figure 19-5) is completely closed to jet aircraft. Even propeller planes have a hard time taking off and landing because the runway has hills on one side and sheer cliffs on the other.

Regardless of the difficult terrain, Saba is a great place to visit, especially for those island-hopping across the Caribbean.

| Specification | Value |
| --- | --- |
| Year opened | 1963 |
| Airport type | Public |
| Airport codes | IATA: SAB |
| | ICAO: TNCS |
| Elevation | 18 m/60 ft |
| Coordinates | 17°38'44"N |
| | 063°13'14"W |

**FIGURE 19-5:**
Juancho
E. Yrausquin
Airport.

# Marble Canyon Airport; Marble Canyon, Arizona, USA

The Grand Canyon is one of the United States' best-known natural wonders, and nothing better than an air tour to let you drink in its majesty. Our choice of departure for buzzing about the Grand Canyon and Arizona desert is Marble Canyon Airport, shown in Figure 19-6.

FIGURE 19-6:
Marble Canyon
Airport.

This strip has one relatively small runway (down the middle in Figure 19-6) that features a rough but well-maintained asphalt surface. You can use this intermediate-skill airport for practice landings, and it gives you a good starting or endpoint for a virtual tour of the American Southwest.

| Specification | Value |
| --- | --- |
| Year opened | 1948 |
| Airport type | Public |
| Airport codes | IATA: MYH |
| | FAA ID: L41 |
| Elevation | 1098 m/3603 ft |
| Coordinates | 36°48'41"N |
| | 111°38'38"W |

# Mataveri International Airport; Easter Island, Chile

Mataveri International Airport, shown in Figure 19-7, is the gateway to the iconic Easter Island. It's the most remote airport in the world, but surprisingly, its runway is quite long (for a remote location) at 3,318 meters (10,885 ft).

FIGURE 19-7:
Mataveri
International
Airport.

The long, well-maintained runway allows even wide-bodied jets to land at Mataveri and makes an interesting challenge for pilots who want somewhere unique to take their 747s, 787s, or A320s. Also, stunning Easter Island makes an excellent destination for virtual sightseers.

| Specification | Value |
| --- | --- |
| Year opened | 1967 |
| Airport type | Military/Public |
| Airport codes | IATA: IPC |
|  | ICAO: SCIP |
| Elevation | 69 m/227 ft |
| Coordinates | 27°09'53"S |
|  | 109°25'18"W |

# Tenzing-Hillary Airport; Lukla, Nepal

Aside from being the starting point for those planning to climb Mt. Everest, Tenzing-Hillary Airport (see Figure 19-8) is known for being one of the most dangerous airports in the world. The short and narrow 527-meter (1,729-ft) runway alone makes landing hard enough, but that's not the only difficulty.

**FIGURE 19-8:**
Tenzing-Hillary
Airport.

The landing challenge is enhanced by a steep drop-off on one end of the runway, mountains directly on the other, and an 11.7-percent grade. As a result, only helicopters and STOL (short takeoff and landing) airplanes can use this airport, where landing consists of slamming your aircraft on the ground, holding the brakes, and praying.

| Specification | Value |
| --- | --- |
| Year opened | 1964 |
| Airport type | Public |
| Airport codes | IATA: LUA |
| | ICAO: VNLK |
| Elevation | 2846 m/9337 ft |
| Coordinates | 27°41′16″N |
| | 86°43′53″E |

# Tokyo International Airport; Tokyo, Japan

Tokyo International Airport (commonly known as Haneda Airport and shown in Figure 19-9) is the fourth-busiest airport globally and is many tourists' first destination in Japan. Japan's varied architecture and environment make it a wonderful country to tour via the air.

**FIGURE 19-9:**
Tokyo
International
Airport.

Beginning your journey at Tokyo International gives a great urban contrast to the rural areas farther out. It also makes a good starting point to see the material added in the Flight Simulator World Update 1: Japan (which you can read about in Chapter 10).

| Specification | Value |
| --- | --- |
| Year opened | 1931 |
| Airport type | Public |
| Airport codes | IATA: HND |
| | ICAO: RJTT |
| Elevation | 6 m/21 ft |
| Coordinates | 35°33′12″N |
| | 139°46′52″E |

# Your Airport

Although many people immediately fly to their house in Flight Simulator, visiting your nearby airport can be just as exciting. Instead of being just a passenger at an airport near you, pay a virtual visit to see things — such as the runway and hangars shown in Figure 19-10 — from a new viewpoint. Doing so can give you some perspective on what it takes to get you into the air in real life.

**FIGURE 19-10:**
The sky's
the limit.

# 7

# Appendixes: Example Flights

Take a simple flight in Microsoft Flight Simulator 2020 with a Textron Aviation Cessna 152.

Fly a twin engine Beechcraft Baron G58 for a slightly more complex Flight Simulator experience.

Move your Flight Simulator experience into the big leagues by flying a Boeing 787 Dreamliner.

# Appendix A

# Example Cessna Flight

The Textron Aviation Cessna 152 is one of the simpler aircraft in Microsoft Flight Simulator 2020. It's the plane you fly in the in-game tutorials and may likely be the first plane you take out on a flight after completing the tutorial. However, this common use doesn't mean it's an easy machine to master. By following along with the instructions in this appendix, you can know what to expect and be prepared for your maiden voyage in a Cessna 152.

This appendix covers a flight from a cold and dark departure until you park at your destination. By this point, you probably know most (if not all) of these concepts, but this appendix puts them all together for you.

## Making a Cold and Dark Start

A *cold and dark start,* which means starting a plane that has been parked for a while, requires that you go through the entire preflight checklist. Starting from a parked position is one of the best ways to familiarize yourself with an aircraft's cockpit because it requires you to use switches and buttons that are located throughout the cabin. The Cessna's cockpit and control panel (see Figure A-1) are relatively simple, and the basics of the start-up sequence are similar on every aircraft.

**FIGURE A-1:**
The Cessna
control panel.

**TIP**

If you decide that you don't want to begin from a cold and dark start — or if you're simply in a hurry — you can autostart the plane instead. Hold down Left Ctrl+E on your keyboard to perform an autostart.

When you *spawn* (load into the game) into the airport of your choice, you can pull up the game's built-in checklist to get started. The in-game checklist for the Cessna is decent, but not every aircraft's checklist is up to the same standards in Flight Simulator. Some checklists give you detailed start-up instructions and steps for each part of the flight, while others give you the bare minimum to get the engines started. Several planes don't offer any kind of checklist, so you're on your own with those.

From the parking area, get the aircraft ready to taxi by making sure you're in cockpit view. If you have any trouble following the steps, note that you can click on the eye icon in the in-game checklist and it directs you to whatever lever, button, or switch you need to activate:

1. **Open the Fuel Shutoff Valve on the floor near the pilot's seat.**

2. **Check that the parking brake is set.**

3. **Set the fuel mixture to rich (100%).**

4. **Set the carburetor heat to Cold (0%).**

5. **Prime the engine twice.**

   To prime the engine, you push the primer button.

6. **Open the throttle 1/2 an inch.**

   This opening equals around 20 percent of the total length between the idle and maximum throttle settings.

7. **Turn on the Battery Master Switch and Alternator Master Switch.**

8. **Turn the ignition to the Start position.**

9. **Adjust the throttle until the engine is revving at 1,000 RPM.**

10. **Ensure the oil pressure stays in the green while the engine warms up.**

    If you notice a drop in pressure, you can throttle up and try to get it back up before the engine shuts down.

11. **Turn on the beacon and navigation lights.**

At this point, the aircraft is prepared to taxi.

# Taxiing Your Cessna 152 for Takeoff

After your Cessna 152 is powered and ready to take off (as shown in Figure A-2), you need to get a piece of valuable information from your local Automatic Terminal Information Service (ATIS), which you can read all about in Chapter 13. Tune into the information channel on your radio by selecting the correct channel from the ATC window and check the local altimeter pressure. Input this information by using the dial located on the altimeter. This is an essential step for aircraft like the Cessna that don't have a Radar Altimeter device, especially if you're planning to fly an Instrument Flight Rules (IFR) plan. (I go over what an IFR entails in Chapter 13.)

Before you can taxi, you need to get permission to do so. For this flight, you're flying VFR (Visual Flight Rules; see Chapter 13), so you need to tune your radio to air traffic control (ATC) clearance (you find this frequency by looking at the ATC window) and request taxi instructions. Tell the air traffic controller the direction of your departure (check your map by clicking on the map icon in the top bar if you don't already know your departure direction).

When you contact the ATC for taxi clearance and instructions, they give you the route through the airport that you must take to the runway. When I practiced this flight, I received this transmission:

Cessna N177AB, taxi to and hold short of runway 35L via taxiway L M cross runway 29 B F A C. Contact tower on 124.2 when ready.

FIGURE A-2:
A Cessna
preparing
to taxi.

These instructions mean that you need to take the following route steps:

1. From where you're parked, take taxiway L.

2. Turn onto taxiway M when you see it.

3. Stay on taxiway M and cross runway 29 when you reach it.

4. Turn onto taxiway B, then F, then A, and then C.

5. Hold at the line just before runway 35L.

6. After you reach the hold line, contact the tower on the frequency provided (in this case, frequency 124.2) and request permission for takeoff.

7. When you receive approval, move onto the runway and stop at the takeoff line.

# Taking Off and Flying a Cessna 152

Taking off can be one of the easier parts of flying. While you're stopped at the takeoff line (which you get to with approval from ATC, as discussed in the preceding section), run a quick check of your Cessna 152 to ensure that everything is configured correctly. You make this quick check by following the takeoff portion of your checklist. After you're satisfied that your airplane is ready to go, throttle up to 100%, head down the runway, and lift off the ground (see in Figure A-3).

The Cessna 152 is a pretty slow aircraft, but you don't need much speed to take off. With 10 degrees of flaps, the plane can take off at a knots-indicated airspeed (KIAS) of 54, and it has a (ridiculously low) stall speed of 40 KIAS. So, you can take off and fly this plane pretty easily, as long as you don't try to climb too fast.

After you take off, follow these steps to maintain a steady climb to the desired altitude:

1. **Raise your flaps (press F5 on a keyboard or LB on a controller).**

2. **Monitor your rate of climb and adjust your yoke to keep the plane steady.**

   Keep your angle of attack in the high green or low yellow area of the attitude indicator.

3. **Trim out the plane by adjusting the elevator trim knob (press Ctrl+Num 7 or Ctrl+Num 1 on a keyboard, or Y+DPAD Up or Y+DPAD Down on controller).**

   Setting the trim keeps your plane in a steady climb without the need to constantly hold the yoke back.

REMEMBER

ATC lets you know what altitude you need to match, and you just need to follow their instructions while you head to your destination. Flying VFR in a Cessna 152 pretty much involves going in a straight line, which makes for a reasonably stress-free trip.

# Landing Your Cessna 152

When you get within radio distance of your destination airport, you can request a landing clearance. You may have the choice of more than one runway, which can confuse things if you're unfamiliar with the airport. If you're not sure which runway to head towards, you can turn on the landing path display in the AI Assist by opening the Assistance panel in the top bar. You still control the landing, but this display gives you a clear indicator of how to make the approach.

Landing is trickier than takeoff, but the Cessna is very forgiving. After you choose a runway and are *inbound* (see the plane in Figure A-4), make sure to continue notifying ATC of what leg of the landing you're currently flying. See Chapter 9 for a discussion of the legs in an airport landing pattern.

**FIGURE A-4:**
A Cessna coming in for a landing.

Follow these steps while you come in for the landing:

1. **Bleed off speed while you make your decent by lowering your engine revolutions per minute (RPMs) or increasing your drag.**

   Reduce your throttle or introduce degrees of flaps as needed. Find the controls for the trim settings (such as flaps) in the earlier section "Taking Off and Flying a Cessna 152."

   **TIP**

   With flaps up, you can land at around 60 to 70 KIAS. However, if you're coming in too fast, you can deploy flaps to use as a pseudo-airbrake. Just make sure you don't accidentally get under your stall speed of 40 KIAS.

2. **After you touch down on the runway, hit your brakes, cut your throttle, and be ready to begin your taxi.**

3. **Pull off on the nearest taxiway and head toward general parking if ATC hasn't given you a particular route.**

   If ATC gives you a route to general parking, follow it.

4. **When you reach general parking, find an empty space with a *pushback tug* (which is the cart used to help airplanes reverse out of parking spaces).**

   An airport flagger should guide you into a parking spot.

5. **Set the parking brake, cut the fuel, and turn off your electronics to end the flight.**

# Appendix **B**

# Example Baron G58 Twin-Engine Flight

The Beechcraft Baron G58 is a beginner-level, twin-engine plane. Although it's more complex than the Cessna 152 (featured in Appendix A), it still uses piston-driven engines and flies at relatively slow speeds compared to its turboprop peers, such as the Beechcraft King Air 350i. (Chapter 12 gives you the lowdown on types of aircraft and their properties.) The Baron G58 is an excellent aircraft choice if you want to move to something a little bigger than a Cessna but are still growing your confidence in your flying prowess.

## Making the Cold and Dark Start in a Beechcraft Baron

The Beechcraft Baron's cold and dark start-up is similar to the Cessna 152's (which you can read about in Appendix A). The most significant differences are that the Baron has two engines, rather than one, and it has a much more complicated all-digital avionics system which requires you to learn how to navigate the Garmin software.

Luckily, the Beechcraft Baron G58 has one of the better flight checklists in the game. If you're familiar with the Cessna 152, many of the controls are in the same spot in the Baron G58. Figure B-1 shows the control panel for the Baron.

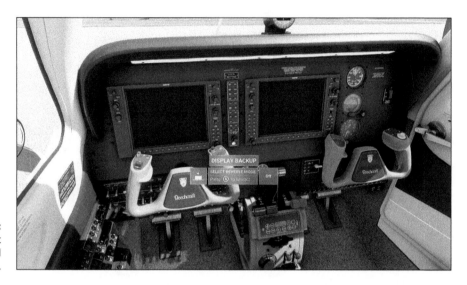

The checklist starts with a *preflight inspection* (a thorough examination of the mechanical parts of an aircraft), which you can do if you're looking for the full role-playing experience. However, the plane *spawns* (loads up in the game) with all the controls configured correctly for a cold and dark start-up, so don't feel bad about skipping that preflight inspection.

To get the plane ready to taxi, you need to follow these steps:

1. **Set a number of controls to the On position.**

   Turn all of these controls on:

   - Both Tank Fuel Control levels

   - Both Alternators

   - The Electric Master switch, which you find beside the yoke.

   - The Strobe Light

   - The left Engine Master switch

   Watch the screen and wait for L ENGINE GLOW to disappear.

2. **Press and hold the Left Engine Start button on the control panel until the engine fires up.**

   Wait until the left engine idles at around 710 RPM.

3. **Repeat the Step 2 sequence for the right engine.**

4. **Turn the Avionic Master switch to the On position.**

   The Beechcraft Baron aircraft is now ready to taxi.

# Taxiing Your Twin-Engine Baron

The Baron is pretty nimble on the ground, as shown in Figure B-1, so you can easily control it while taxiing. However, it doesn't have a reverser (which means you can't back up), so you need to call for pushback if you don't have sufficient space to turn out of your parking spot.

FIGURE B-2:
A Beechcraft Baron preparing to taxi.

REMEMBER

Because the Baron has a full avionics suite that includes radar, an autopilot, and navigational software, you can choose between a Visual Flight Rules (VFR) or Instrument Flight Rules (IFR) flight plan. The information you get from ATC differs depending on which set of flight rules you follow, so make sure to copy down the briefing information. (See Chapter 13 for more on briefings and other flight information.)

If you're using an IFR flight plan, the information you confirmed on the World Map should have automatically been entered. If not (or if you decide to go somewhere else) enter it properly into your flight computer and double-check by looking at the new route on your map. Also, familiarize yourself with the bearings associated with each *waypoint* (an intermediate point along the travel route) in your journey.

After you get your flight plan squared away, call ATC ground (a frequency that you can find by checking the radio panel) for taxi instructions. Follow those instructions to the runway.

# Taking Off and Flying the Baron

Taking off in the Beechcraft Baron isn't much more complicated than in the Cessna 152 (see Figure B-3). (Check out Appendix A for more about taking off in the Cessna.) Of course, you need to turn your radio to the ATC tower frequency and ask for permission to take off. *Note:* You do need to make sure that both engines on your Baron stay synched by advancing the throttles together so that the plane stays straight when moving down the runway.

The Baron doesn't need a long runway to make it into the air. After you accelerate to around 100 knots-indicated airspeed (KIAS), you can *rotate* (pitch the nose up by pulling back on the yoke) and start your climb.

**FIGURE B-3:**
A Beechcraft
Baron
lifting off.

**REMEMBER**

During flight, remember to follow any instructions from ATC, such as altitude and heading, that apply to your flight plan and route.

# Landing in the Beechcraft Baron

Landings in a twin-engine plane (as shown in Figure B-4) can be a bit harder to pull off than landings in a single-engine craft. For example, you touch down at a faster speed in a Baron G58 than you do in a Cessna 152, which can make slowing and stopping more difficult. However, the Baron still has a reasonably low stall speed of 73 KIAS, so beginner pilots have plenty of cushion to play with approach speed before worrying that the plane may drop out of the sky.

**FIGURE B-4:** A Beechcraft Baron approaching for landing.

**TIP**

The most common issue to watch for when landing a multi-engine plane is *slewing*, which affects the position of the aircraft related to the landing surface. Even minor variations in RPM between the engines can cause the aircraft to drift right or left when you touch down. Be ready to compensate for this movement by adjusting the rudder and front wheel.

After you land the Baron and slow down to around 20 knots, you're on easy street. Just follow the taxi instructions that you receive from ATC ground (if you have them) or take the first taxiway off the runway and locate your parking area.

# Appendix C

# Example 787 Dreamliner Flight

After you work through this example, consider yourself in the big league. Flying a Boeing 787 Dreamliner is a huge task compared to handling the single and dual prop aircraft presented in Appendixes A and B. However, the principles of flight that you use in those examples (and throughout the book) still apply here.

Most of the challenge associated with flying this plane comes from its enormous size. For example, the 787's mass makes it harder to slow down and unwieldy to maneuver. But you can expect every aspect of piloting this flight to be more complex and harder to perform than when you're flying smaller planes.

## Starting Cold and Dark in the 787

Although the Dreamliner fundamentally works on the same principles as any other plane, the cold and dark start-up sequence is dramatically different from that of a Cessna 152 (see Appendix A). Most of the action takes place on the overhead panel, shown in Figure C-1. You have to deal with advanced concepts such as the Auxiliary Power Unit (APU) and ground/external power.

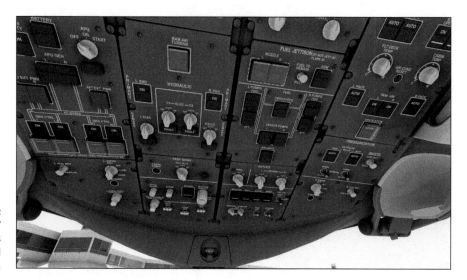

**FIGURE C-1:**
The Boeing 787
Dreamliner's
overhead
control panel.

Unfortunately, the 787 has one of the *worst* checklists you find in Microsoft Flight Simulator 2020, and many of the functions that exist on the real plane aren't modeled in the game. However, the basics are here, and you can acquire certain mods that give you access to a more complex and realistic simulation of the aircraft.

To begin getting ready to taxi, follow these steps:

1. **On the overhead control panel, turn the battery switch to the On position.**

2. **Activate external power by pressing the Left and Right FWD External Power switches and the Aft External Power switch.**

3. **Start the APU and wait for it to spool up.**

   You know that spooling is complete when the APU gauge on the flight systems panel stops increasing.

4. **Turn the Left and Right APU GEN (short for generator) switches to the On position.**

5. **Turn the fuel pumps to the On position.**

6. **Activate the beacon by pressing the Beacon button on the overhead control panel.**

7. **Contact air traffic control (ATC) to receive your Instrument Flight Rules (IFR) clearance and the altitude assignment.**

   You get the ATC radio frequency automatically via the ATC panel.

8. **Reset the altimeter to correct air pressure, which you get by contacting ATIS on the radio.**

9. **Enter your first altitude assignment into the Altitude Hold panel.**

10. **Arm the autothrottle (A/T), lateral navigation (LNAV), vertical navigation (VNAV), and Flight Director to prepare the autopilot.**

    You find these settings on the autopilot panel above the flight information displays.

11. **Set the throttles to idle.**

    They're in the idle position by default.

12. **Activate the right engine starter on the overhead control panel and set the right engine fuel control to Run by flipping the switch to the rear of the throttle quadrant.**

    Wait for the right engine's RPMs to stabilize; you can recognize stabilization when the RPMs stop increasing.

13. **Repeat the process in Step 12 to start the left engine.**

14. **Call the local ground channel, which you find in the ATC panel by using the radio.**

15. **Select the option to push back from the gate.**

16. **After pushback, turn the APU to the Off position and turn on the required external lights by pressing the appropriate buttons on the overhead control panel. Then, deactivate the APU generators.**

17. **Get taxi clearance from the ATC ground by choosing the correct selection from the ATC menu.**

# Taxiing Your Dreamliner

I can't overstate the fact that the 787 is a big beast. When you taxi (as depicted in Figure C-2), the 787's turns are wide, and you really need to anticipate each turn in advance. You also need to be very careful when crossing runways because the Dreamliner takes a lot longer to clear them.

Even just moving is a bit tougher. The engines on the 787 provide a lot of thrust, and a little goes a long way. Give the aircraft sufficient time to build momentum and get moving when you increase the throttle. Otherwise, you quickly find yourself speeding past the 20-knot speed limit for ground traffic.

After you make it to the runway, like with any plane, hold short and contact ATC on the tower control frequency that you find in the ATC panel. Then ask for permission to take off.

# Taking Off and Flying the 787

The Dreamliner requires more runway to get up to speed than most aircraft in the game, which means it's limited to operating out of larger airfields. It must also achieve almost double the speed of a Cessna or Beechcraft Baron (around 135–150 knots) to take off. Figure C-3 shows a Dreamliner on the runway.

You can engage the autopilot directly after liftoff, and the settings should be automatic based on your flight plan (see Chapter 13 about flight plans). The plane can fly to its destination with minimum input from you.

FIGURE C-3:
A 787 taking
flight.

# Landing Your Big Boat — er, Plane

Landing in the 787 (on approach in Figure C-4) is made easier by the fact that you can make most of the descent by using the autopilot. You'll be able to see each waypoint and your landing runway in the World Map screen.

FIGURE C-4:
A Boeing 787
Dreamliner
landing.

When you radio in to request permission to land, the ATC gives you a landing runway and tells you which waypoint you need to take to get there. ATC uses waypoints to route traffic around the airspace immediately around the airport. You also need to enter the ILS frequency — which you find by looking at your target's airport diagram — and plug it in on the flight computer (if it doesn't automatically populate). You can also enter your assigned runway and waypoint into the flight computer, and the plane begins descending via autopilot.

REMEMBER

Even though autopilot helps you descend, you must do the actual landing yourself. When you get low enough (an altitude of about 500 ft above the runway), disengage the autopilot and touch down. The 787 has a reverser, which you engage by pulling the throttles to idle and then continuing to hold the decrease throttle button. Use the reverser in conjunction with your brakes to slow the aircraft.

After you decelerate to around 20 knots (taxiing speed), you can follow taxi instructions from ATC ground and move off the runway toward your gate.

# Index

# B

base leg, of approach patterns, 121
Basic Controls modules (Flight Training), 40
Beechcraft Baron G58, 167, 257–261
Beechcraft King Air 350i, 163
beginners, airplanes for, 165
Bloom setting (VR Mode), 61
Boeing (United States), 161
Boeing 747-8 Intercontinental airliner, 161
Boeing 787 Dreamliner, 161, 166, 263–268
Bombardier Aerospace (Canada), 161
Bombardier CRJ550ER, 172, 173
Bora Bora (French Polynesia) Discovery Flight, 38
brakes, keybinds for, 28, 33
Buildings setting (VR Mode), 60
Bush Trips (Activities), 41

# C

call sign, changing, 233–234
Call Sign option, 70
calling up the radio, 188–190
camera mode switches, keybinds for, 26, 33
cameras, keybinds for, 24–26, 32–33
cargo, allowing for with flight plans, 178–179
center of gravity (CG), 178
centering, on runways, 108
Cessna 152, 94, 95, 102, 112, 165, 204, 218, 249–255
Cessna 172 Skyhawk, 42, 94
Cessna 208 B Grand Caravan EX, 168
Cessna Citation CJ4, 102, 162
Cessna Citation Longitude, 162, 166
CFR (Code of Federal Regulations), 194
CG (center of gravity), 178
changing
  approach for emergency landings, 217–218
  ATC call sign, 233–234
  descent, 122
  game performance settings for VR Mode, 59–61
  making before takeoff, 44–45
  sim rate, 230–231

Cheat Sheet (website), 4
checking flaps, before takeoff, 107–108
Checklist Assist setting, 90
Checklist in UI Panel open at start assist, 89
choosing
  airplanes, 160
  altitude, 174–175
  arrival airports, 137–138, 172–173
  departure airports, 137, 172–173
  departure points for multiplayer sessions, 65–66
  destinations for multiplayer sessions, 71–72
  flight rules, 171–172
  instrument flight rules (IFR), 171–172
  manual control or autopilot for multiplayer sessions, 72
  Microsoft Flight Simulator, 14–18
  starter planes, 102
  visual flight rules (VFR), 171–172
  waypoints, 172–173
City Markers assist, 89
climbing, maintaining speed while, 116–117
cockpit camera, keybinds for, 24, 32
cockpits
  custom, 20–22
  running with controllers, 31–34
  running with keyboards, 22–31
Code of Federal Regulations (CFR), 194
cold and dark start
  Beechcraft Baron G58, 257–259
  Boeing 787 Dreamliner, 263–265
  Textron Aviation Cessna 152, 249–251
collaborating cross-console, in multiplayer sessions, 73–75
commit-to-fly ($V_1$) speed, 110
communicating
  with air traffic control (ATC) rules, 147–148
  with air traffic control (ATC) sequence, 148–156
  with air traffic control (ATC) while in the air, 154–155
  communication platform for multiplayer sessions, 66
  continuously with air traffic control (ATC), 146
  using radio, 190

complete failure, 203

computing equipment, verifying requirements for VR, 53

consoles

about, 20

instruments on, 183

troubleshooting connectivity for multiplayer sessions, 75

Contact Shadows setting (VR Mode), 61

Control Aircraft setting, 91

control trimming surfaces, keybinds for, 29, 34

controllers, running cockpits with, 31–34

controls

about, 19

custom setups/cockpits, 20–22

PC, 21

running cockpit from keyboard, 22–31

running cockpit with controller, 31–34

correcting

alignment, 115–116

vertical stabilization, 115–116

cost, of implementing VR, 51

Courchevel Altiport (French Alps), 236–237

course, finding your, 114–115

Crash Damage assist, 87, 88

creating

groups for multiplayer sessions, 64–65

itineraries for multiplayer sessions, 66–72

cross-console, collaborating in multiplayer sessions, 73–75

crosswind, 111

crosswind leg, of approach patterns, 121

current heading, 93

Current Heading indicator, in analog cockpit, 96

Current Navigational Data, on multifunction flight display (MFD), 99

custom setups/cockpits, 20–22

customizing pilot avatar, 232–233

cutting off aircraft, 197

cylinder failure, 203

## D

Daher TBM 930, 162, 167

Deluxe Edition

about, 15–16

handcrafted airports, 141

departure airports

evaluating, 103–105

selecting, 137, 172–173

departure approval, getting, 150–151

departure points, selecting for multiplayer sessions, 65–66

descent, adjusting, 122

designations, of runways, 132

destinations, selecting for multiplayer sessions, 71–72

determining

emergencies, 202–203

emergency landing locations, 215–217

Discord app, 66

Discovery Flights, 36–38

Distance and Course indicator, on primary flight display (PFD), 98

DME, keybinds for, 30

downward pitch, avoiding, 116

downwind leg, of approach patterns, 120

drag, 85–86

drone camera

about, 229–230

keybinds for, 25, 32

Dubai International Airport (Dubai, United Arab Emirates), 237–238

## E

early landings, 207

electrical failures, managing, 208–209

electrics, keybinds for, 24

elevators, controlling, 82

Embraer (Brazil), 161

emergencies. See also emergency landings

about, 201

adapting to continue flights, 206

determining, 202–203

landings. *See also* emergency landings

  about, 119–120

  acquiring instructions for, 155–156

  adjusting descent, 122

  approach patterns, 120–122

  Beechcraft Baron G58, 261

  Boeing 787 Dreamliner, 267–268

  landing early, 207

  monitoring airspeed, 122–123

  monitoring RPM, 122–123

  practicing safe, 46–47

  smooth, 123–124

  taxi instructions, 125

  Textron Aviation Cessna 152, 254–255

  touching down, 123–125

landmarks

  emergency landings and, 219

  heading to/from popular, 105–106

lateral axis, 80–81

lift

  defined, 85

  effect of inclination on, 118

Light Shafts setting (VR Mode), 61

lights, keybinds for, 30–31

listening

  knowing what to listen for, 189

  for other aircraft, 189–190

Liveries option, 69–70

locations, determining for emergency landings, 215–217

Lockheed P-38 Lightning aircraft, 149

long-haul flights, airplanes for, 166

longitudinal axis, 83

# M

magnetic direction, 132

magneto left, 203

magneto right, 203

Main Menu

  about, 35–36

  Activities, 41

Discovery Flights, 36–38

Flight Training, 39–40

Marketplace, 41

tabs on, 36

World Map, 38–39

maintaining

  contact with air traffic control (ATC) while in the air, 154–155

  speed while climbing, 116–117

making turns, 118

Manage Radio Comms setting, 91

managing

  adverse weather conditions, 110–112

  cockpits with controllers, 31–34

  cockpits with keyboards, 22–31

  electrical failures, 208–209

  elevators, 82

  engine failures, 209–210

  equipment failures, 208–210

manual controls, selecting for multiplayer sessions, 72

Marble Canyon Airport (Marble Canyon, Arizona, USA), 241–242

Maria Reiche Neuman Airport (SPZA), 105–106

Marketplace, 41

Mataveri International Airport (Easter Island, Chile), 242–243

Max Allowable Fuel, 178, 179

Max Payload, 179

Maximum Takeoff Weight, 179

mean sea level (MSL), 195

menu commands, keybinds for, 26–27

Meta (Oculus) Quest 2, 56–57

MFD (multifunction flight display), 99

Microsoft Flight Simulator. *See also specific topics*

  evaluating benefits of, 13–14

  evolution of, 10–13

  purchasing, 14–18

  releases of, 12

  selecting, 14–18

  versions, 15–17

Microsoft Xbox voice chat, 66

midair starts, 224–225

# X

Xbox, as a platform for Microsoft Flight
Simulator, 15

XPNDR, keybinds for, 30

# Y

yaw, 80, 82–83

yoke, 81, 96

# About the Author

**Brittany Vincent** is an accomplished video game, technology, and entertainment writer and editor whose work has been featured in various online and print publications. She's been writing professionally for 15 years and enjoys combining her extensive video game knowledge with her passion for the written word. To date, she's written hundreds of articles surrounding gaming and every adjacent topic.

Her work can be found in dozens of print and digital publications such as *CNN, The Hollywood Reporter, Variety, Playboy, Rolling Stone, Wired, Maxim, Official Xbox Magazine, PlayStation: The Official Magazine, Hyper Magazine, Otaku USA, PSM3, BuzzFeed, Eurogamer, Engadget, AskMen, Tom's Guide, Laptop Magazine, GameSpot, IGN, GamesRadar*, and many more.

Brittany has attended video game conventions, including PAX East and E3, as a reporter and panelist. She's also provided expert commentary for major news organizations such as NPR and ABC. Now, she's written her debut book and hopes there are many more on the way.

Outside of writing, Brittany collects video games and consoles, from the Philips CD-I to the Casio Loopy, and everything in between. She also loves anime, the '80s and '90s, and Care Bears. See her body of work at www.brittanyvincent.com and feel free to get in touch via Twitter: @MolotovCupcake.

# Dedication

To my fiancé JF, who never stopped encouraging me to fly higher. I love you more than anything in this world. First stop, a new couch. Next stop, a house. I'm joking, we'll never be able to buy a house in *this* economy. But who needs those things when we have each other?

# Author's Acknowledgments

To my friend and colleague Josh, thank you for your endless support and your willingness to drop everything and assist me. You're a consummate professional and an even better writer.

To my sister Katie, thanks for being there for every laugh, every meltdown, and every hoard of Glade Plug-Ins in my bathroom closet. I owe you a pile of mini backpacks for your kindness and patience and I appreciate you and your beautiful family so, so much.

Thank you to everyone who answered an e-mail, shot me a text, or otherwise offered assistance while this book was in progress.

To those who still insist in 2023 that women don't play video games, we do. And this one has been playing for nearly 25 years. *You're welcome.*

## Publisher's Acknowledgments

**Executive Editor:** Steve Hayes

**Project Manager and Development Editor:**
Leah Michael

**Copy Editor:** Laura K. Miller

**Technical Editor:** Jason Faulkner

**Production Editor:** Tamilmani Varadharaj

**Cover Image:** © Kletr/Shutterstock

# Take dummies with you everywhere you go!

Whether you are excited about e-books, want more from the web, must have your mobile apps, or are swept up in social media, dummies makes everything easier.

**Find us online!**

# dummies.com

# Leverage the power

*Dummies* is the global leader in the reference category and one of the most trusted and highly regarded brands in the world. No longer just focused on books, customers now have access to the dummies content they need in the format they want. Together we'll craft a solution that engages your customers, stands out from the competition, and helps you meet your goals.

## Advertising & Sponsorships

Connect with an engaged audience on a powerful multimedia site, and position your message alongside expert how-to content. Dummies.com is a one-stop shop for free, online information and know-how curated by a team of experts.

- Targeted ads
- Video
- Email Marketing
- Microsites
- Sweepstakes sponsorship

**20 MILLION** PAGE VIEWS EVERY SINGLE MONTH

**15 MILLION UNIQUE** VISITORS PER MONTH

**43%** OF ALL VISITORS ACCESS THE SITE VIA THEIR MOBILE DEVICES

**700,000** NEWSLETTER SUBSCRIPTIONS TO THE INBOXES OF
*300,000* UNIQUE INDIVIDUALS EVERY WEEK

# of dummies

## Custom Publishing

Reach a global audience in any language by creating a solution that will differentiate you from competitors, amplify your message, and encourage customers to make a buying decision.

- Apps
- Books
- eBooks
- Video
- Audio
- Webinars

## Brand Licensing & Content

Leverage the strength of the world's most popular reference brand to reach new audiences and channels of distribution.

## For more information, visit dummies.com/biz

# PERSONAL ENRICHMENT

9781119187790
USA $26.00
CAN $31.99
UK £19.99

9781119179030
USA $21.99
CAN $25.99
UK £16.99

9781119293354
USA $24.99
CAN $29.99
UK £17.99

9781119293347
USA $22.99
CAN $27.99
UK £16.99

9781119310068
USA $22.99
CAN $27.99
UK £16.99

9781119235606
USA $24.99
CAN $29.99
UK £17.99

9781119251163
USA $24.99
CAN $29.99
UK £17.99

9781119235491
USA $26.99
CAN $31.99
UK £19.99

9781119279952
USA $24.99
CAN $29.99
UK £17.99

9781119283133
USA $24.99
CAN $29.99
UK £17.99

9781119287117
USA $24.99
CAN $29.99
UK £16.99

9781119130246
USA $22.99
CAN $27.99
UK £16.99

# PROFESSIONAL DEVELOPMENT

9781119311041
USA $24.99
CAN $29.99
UK £17.99

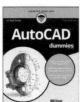
9781119255796
USA $39.99
CAN $47.99
UK £27.99

9781119293439
USA $26.99
CAN $31.99
UK £19.99

9781119281467
USA $26.99
CAN $31.99
UK £19.99

9781119280651
USA $29.99
CAN $35.99
UK £21.99

9781119251132
USA $24.99
CAN $29.99
UK £17.99

9781119310563
USA $34.00
CAN $41.99
UK £24.99

9781119181705
USA $29.99
CAN $35.99
UK £21.99

9781119263593
USA $26.99
CAN $31.99
UK £19.99

9781119257769
USA $29.99
CAN $35.99
UK £21.99

9781119293477
USA $26.99
CAN $31.99
UK £19.99

9781119265313
USA $24.99
CAN $29.99
UK £17.99

9781119239314
USA $29.99
CAN $35.99
UK £21.99

9781119293323
USA $29.99
CAN $35.99
UK £21.99

**dummies.com**

**dummies**
A Wiley Brand

# Learning Made Easy

## ACADEMIC

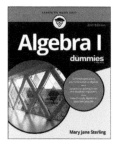

9781119293576
USA $19.99
CAN $23.99
UK £15.99

9781119293637
USA $19.99
CAN $23.99
UK £15.99

9781119293491
USA $19.99
CAN $23.99
UK £15.99

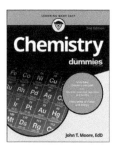

9781119293460
USA $19.99
CAN $23.99
UK £15.99

9781119293590
USA $19.99
CAN $23.99
UK £15.99

9781119215844
USA $26.99
CAN $31.99
UK £19.99

9781119293378
USA $22.99
CAN $27.99
UK £16.99

9781119293521
USA $19.99
CAN $23.99
UK £15.99

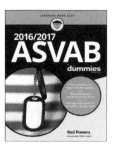

9781119239178
USA $18.99
CAN $22.99
UK £14.99

9781119263883
USA $26.99
CAN $31.99
UK £19.99

## Available Everywhere Books Are Sold

# Small books for big imaginations

9781119177173
USA $9.99
CAN $9.99
UK £8.99

9781119177272
USA $9.99
CAN $9.99
UK £8.99

9781119177241
USA $9.99
CAN $9.99
UK £8.99

9781119177210
USA $9.99
CAN $9.99
UK £8.99

9781119262657
USA $9.99
CAN $9.99
UK £6.99

9781119291336
USA $9.99
CAN $9.99
UK £6.99

9781119233527
USA $9.99
CAN $9.99
UK £6.99

9781119291220
USA $9.99
CAN $9.99
UK £6.99

9781119177302
USA $9.99
CAN $9.99
UK £8.99

## Unleash Their Creativity

**dummies.com**